Central Cambridge

A Guide to the University and Colleges

SECOND EDITION

Kevin Taylor

CAMBRIDGE
UNIVERSITY PRESS
www.cambridge.org

CAMBRIDGE UNIVERSITY PRESS
Cambridge, New York, Melbourne, Madrid, Cape Town, Singapore, São Paulo,
Delhi, Tokyo, Mexico City

Cambridge University Press
The Edinburgh Building, Cambridge CB2 8RU, UK

Published in the United States of America by Cambridge University Press, New York

www.cambridge.org
Information on this title: www.cambridge.org/9780521717182

First edition published 1994 (reprinted 1996, 1997, 1999, 2003, 2004)
Second edition published 2008
Reprinted 2011

Printed in the United Kingdom at the University Press, Cambridge

A catalogue record for this publication is available from the British Library

ISBN 978-0-521-88876-9 Hardback
ISBN 978-0-521-71718-2 Paperback

Contents

Foreword

by H.R.H. The Prince Philip, Duke of Edinburgh,
Chancellor of the University of Cambridge.

BUCKINGHAM PALACE.

Central Cambridge was first published in 1994 in response to the growing number of visitors to the Town and University. Since then there have been numerous re-prints, but this is an entirely updated and expanded version. Cambridge may look as if nothing had changed for centuries, but neither Town nor University have ever stood still. There have been major developments in both since the first edition of *Central Cambridge*.

Cambridge is a remarkable mixture of ancient and modern; town and gown; College communities and academic institutions. It is a product of evolution rather than of deliberate design. There are buildings dating from every stage of its development since the early middle ages. The University and City give it an unique atmosphere as they continue to adapt to changing circumstances, and bring life and meaning to their respective parts of the whole. It is most certainly neither a museum nor a tourist trap.

After some 800 years, the University has become a complex organism, and, for those who have no experience of its contemporary life and activities, a general guide – such as this – is essential to understanding this ancient community and seat of learning, and modern center of research. It describes many of the famous clerics, scholars and builders, who have helped to make its architecture and its history. It also draws a picture of it as a vigorous and energetic part of the educational fabric of our nation, and of the world's academic community as a whole.

Preface and acknowledgements

The first edition of *Central Cambridge: A Guide to the University and Colleges* appeared in 1994. Small-scale updates were made in successive reprints, but this second edition represents the first major overhaul of its content and layout.

The fully revised, updated and redesigned new edition contains freshly commissioned photographs, mainly from the Japanese artist and photographer Hiroshi Shimura; comprehensively updated text, with all facts and figures re-checked, supplemented and updated as appropriate; extensions of the individual college and University entries to incorporate new details and to take account of new buildings; fresh maps, adapted from the latest edition of the official University Map; a significantly extended glossary, further reading section and index; and a new Foreword by the Chancellor, H.R.H. The Prince Philip. Almost every entry in the book has received some update or addition, many of them substantial.

The first edition of the guidebook benefited from the input of numerous individuals including Marcus Askwith, Liesel Boughton-Fox, Christopher Brooke, Bill Davies, Ian Hart, Gordon Johnson, Elisabeth Leedham-Green, Roger Lovatt, Robin Matthews, David McKitterick, Simon Mitton, Jeremy Mynott, Harry Porter, Nicholas Ray, Geoffrey Skelsey, Frank Stubbings, Sarah Taylor, Malcolm Underwood, Robin Walker, Martin Walters, Max Walters and Tony Wilson. Some of the above helped again with this new edition: my thanks go to them, and to the representatives of individual colleges and other parts of the University who checked their revised entries, as well as to Marc Anderson, Rob Beddow, Stephen Bourne, Susan Bowring, Kate Brett, Andrew Brown, Gillian Dadd, Peter Davison, Richard Fisher, Peter Fox, Greg Hayman, Mark Hurn, Alastair Lynn, Alan McArthur, Caroline Murray, Jonathan Nicholls, Peter Raby, Liz Reeve and Stephanie Thelwell for comments and inspiration of various kinds. Chris McLeod of Hart McLeod Ltd deserves a special mention for his layout, design and project-management; and the book is visually strengthened by the photography of Hiroshi Shimura, with whom it has been a great pleasure to work. All photographs in this second edition are by him unless otherwise acknowledged in the captions.

Kevin Taylor
Cambridge University Press

Colleges in the University of Cambridge

Name	Location	Date of foundation	Page	Map ref.
Peterhouse	Trumpington Street	1284	p.57	F 11
Clare College	Trinity Lane	1326	p.18	E 8
Pembroke College	Trumpington Street	1347	p.54	F 10
Gonville and Caius College	Trinity Street	1348	p.30	F 7
Trinity Hall	Trinity Lane	1350	p.21	E 7
Corpus Christi College	Trumpington Street	1352	p.46	F 9
King's College	King's Parade	1441	p.14	F 8
Queens' College	Queens' Lane	1448	p.50	E 10
St Catharine's College	Trumpington Street	1473	p.48	F 9
Jesus College	Jesus Lane	1496	p.79	H 5
Christ's College	St Andrew's Street	1505	p.72	H 7
St John's College	St John's Street	1511	p.36	F 6
Magdalene College	Magdalene Street	1542	p.83	E 4
Trinity College	Trinity Street	1546	p.32	F 6
Emmanuel College	St Andrew's Street	1584	p.70	I 9
Sidney Sussex College	Sidney Street	1596	p.78	G 6
Homerton College	Hills Road	1768	p.104	south-east of I 10
Downing College	Regent Street	1800	p.68	I 10
Girton College	Huntingdon Road	1869	p.99	north of A 1
Newnham College	Sidgwick Avenue	1871	p.88	B 11
Selwyn College	Grange Road	1882	p.90	A 11
Hughes Hall	Mortimer Road	1885	p.103	east of I 9
St Edmund's College	Mount Pleasant	1896	p.95	B 2
New Hall	Huntingdon Road	1954	p.100	B 1
Churchill College	Storey's Way	1960	p.96	west of A 3
Darwin College	Silver Street	1964	p.53	D 11
Lucy Cavendish College	Lady Margaret Road	1965	p.95	C 4
Wolfson College	Barton Road	1965	p.107	west of A 13
Clare Hall	Herschel Road	1966	p.91	west of A 9
Fitzwilliam College	Huntingdon Road	1966	p.100	A 1
Robinson College	Grange Road	1977	p.92	west of A 8

Note

Dates of foundation given are those normally recognised or celebrated within each college. In reality some colleges were founded in the above dates under different names or on different sites from the ones they now have, while others were re-foundations of earlier institutions on the same site, and others were not formally approved by the University until after their date of foundation. Such details are noted within the individual college entries in this guidebook.

Map references here and throughout the book refer to the map on the inside front cover and are keyed to the main entrance of the site in question.

Museums in the University of Cambridge

Introduction

1 Old Schools and Senate-House
from Great St Mary's Church tower

In 2009 the University of Cambridge celebrates its 800th anniversary, the origins of the University dating back to the year 1209. What have those 800 years represented in this place? Through a description of the main University, college and city sites, relating their history to their present appearance and function, this guidebook tells the story of a remarkable institution.

Cambridge itself is a city of just under 125,000 inhabitants, with a history that dates back nearly 2,000 years to Roman times when a small garrison stood on what is now Castle Hill, north-west of the Magdalene Bridge crossing of the River Cam. Advantageously placed at the navigable head of a river network leading to the sea, and only 60 miles north of London by road, it grew as a trading post with several churches. Cambridge's position and character, like those of Oxford 80 miles to the south west, were among the factors which drew to it a number of monasteries, as well as groups of scholars and teachers engaged in the pursuit of knowledge, mainly in the fields of theology, church law, civil (i.e. Roman) law, and logic; and by the year 1209 the makings of a University were in place.

2 Across to St John's from Great St Mary's Church tower

Now, 800 years later, Cambridge is the home of a University which consists of 31 colleges, where students reside, eat, and are taught in small groups; of various faculties, departments, and institutes, where particular subjects are researched, lectured on, or taught; and of administrative and ceremonial buildings. The University of Cambridge has a Library, a Press, an international examinations business, a Botanic Garden, a Business School and eight museums, as well as close connections with four theological colleges, numerous churches, and a major hospital. In total there are about 18,000 full-time students in the University, of whom nearly 12,000 are undergraduates. Some 5,000 students are from overseas, nearly two-thirds of these at postgraduate level, with the most represented countries being the U.S.A. and China (c.700 students each), followed by Germany and Canada. The University employs a total academic, research and support staff of 8,500.

With some notable exceptions, such as the Senate-House, Great St Mary's Church, and the Fitzwilliam Museum, the buildings that attract visitors to Cambridge belong to the colleges. Colleges have existed here since the late thirteenth century, and it is this that distinguishes Cambridge (as well as Oxford) from other, less ancient universities in which control is more centralised. The relationship between the colleges and other parts of the University is an unusual one. A college is a centre of teaching and learning which also acts as a social and residential unit within the University. Every student belongs to a college, and most are provided with food and rooms by their college. However, each of the 31 colleges is self-governing and to a significant extent financially independent, relying not upon central University funding but upon special grants, donations, tuition fees from students, and in the case of the older colleges upon bequests, endowments, and investments that have increased in value over many centuries. The colleges are legally individual private institutions, while the non-collegiate parts of the University form a separate entity, and this inter-dependent combination of private and public spheres has proved to be one of the strengths of the Cambridge system. A college takes responsibility for the admission and general welfare of its undergraduate students, offers teaching for them in groups of a manageable size across the whole range of subject areas, and provides a Director of Studies who supervises their academic pursuits. Colleges also provide libraries, to supplement those available elsewhere in the University.

The college teaching enhances that supplied by the University. Students from all of the colleges attend lectures or go to laboratories which are controlled not by the colleges but by the non-collegiate University via subject-specific units of administration called faculties

3 Processing from the Senate-House

or departments. Thus, a typical student will matriculate (enrol) in the University of Cambridge as an undergraduate to read (study) a particular subject (such as Natural Sciences, or Mathematics, or Classics, or Law) at the age of 18 or 19, having achieved a sufficiently high standard at school level, and that student's life in Cambridge will then be based in his or her college (e.g. King's, or Emmanuel, or New Hall, or Robinson), but will involve regular attendance at the University sites determined by the subject he or she is reading (e.g. at the Department of Pathology, or Department of Engineering, or Faculty of Classics, or Faculty of Law). A student will complete the degree course by passing the requisite University examinations and then graduating in the subject, becoming a graduate.

Postgraduates are students who already hold a first degree and who are now studying for some more advanced purpose, such as a doctorate. They are admitted to courses by the Board of Graduate Studies and their work is based in the University departments. For them, the colleges – which are multidisciplinary – provide a stimulating social and intellectual environment in support of their work.

There are three terms in the Cambridge academic year: the Michaelmas term, running from October to December; the Lent, from January to March; and the Easter, from April to June. An undergraduate course of study in most cases lasts for three years (though a number run for four) and involves an examination known as a tripos, which usually leads to a degree called the Bachelor of Arts (B.A.). Tripos examinations take place in about 30 subject areas, and the results help determine whether a student will receive a first-class, second-class, or third-class degree. By far the most populous tripos course is Natural Sciences (accommodating just over 2,000 undergraduates in total), with Medicine, Engineering, Mathematics, Law, Modern & Medieval Languages, English and History following in that order. Economics, Veterinary Medicine, Social & Political Sciences, Education Studies and Geography also attract student numbers in excess of 300. Since the abolition of the Cambridge Entrance Examination in 1985, admission is usually now determined by performance in national school exams such as 'A' Levels, and by interview.

The date of 1209 provides a marker for the origin of the University of Cambridge, for in that year groups of scholars (reputedly migrants from the University of Oxford, which existed slightly earlier) had begun to congregate here for the purpose of study. Teaching in those early days revolved around theological subjects, and a close relationship between the church and University existed for several hundred years. At least four of Cambridge's surviving medieval churches served at various times as college chapels.

4 Lady Elizabeth de Clare, foundress of Clare College, and Lady Margaret Beaufort, foundress of Christ's and St John's Colleges

(from Ackermann's *A History of the University of Cambridge*, 1815: images courtesy of Cambridge University Library)

The college system, modelled on those at Paris and Oxford, began in 1284 with the foundation of Peterhouse, and by 1400 seven of the present-day colleges existed in some form (including Trinity, which did not adopt its modern identity until 1546). The number had risen to 17 by 1800; and in the nineteenth century the University itself underwent a rapid expansion, partly in response to the rise of science in a fast-changing world. In the twentieth century 14 additional colleges were formally affiliated to the University – some of them Victorian institutions newly recognised, others new foundations. The 14 included a college for mature women (Lucy Cavendish), and five 'graduate colleges' intended mainly for postgraduates and mature students (Clare Hall, Darwin, Hughes Hall, St Edmund's and Wolfson). This brings the total to 31, ranging in size from Homerton, with around 1,100 students, to Lucy Cavendish and Clare Hall, with fewer than 200 each.

Each college has its own atmosphere and traditions. Some are more relaxed, others more formal. A number preserve traditions such as a nightly dinner at which gowns are worn and a Latin grace recited; a system of Scholarships and Exhibitions to enhance the status of undergraduates who perform well; and an emphasis on accommodating the majority of students within the main college buildings to help them feel members of a tight-knit community.

Only 26 of the colleges have the word 'College' in their familiar title. Four retain the word 'Hall' instead, and then there is Peterhouse. The heads of the colleges also go by different titles, ranging from Master (the most common), to President (six colleges), Principal (two), Mistress (one), Provost (one), and Warden (one).

The picturesque quality of the central colleges is enhanced by their position on the river, which runs from south to north past Darwin, Queens', King's, Clare, Trinity Hall, Trinity, St John's, and Magdalene. These colleges back on to the riverbank, giving rise to the name the

Backs, which describes this thousand-metre stretch. Here the river is known as the Cam, but at various times in history it has been called the Granta, a word which now designates a small tributary of the Cam and which is familiar from the name of Grantchester village, a two-and-a-half-mile walk away along delightful meadow paths to the south.

Two of the earliest Cambridge colleges (Michaelhouse, 1324; and King's Hall, 1337) no longer exist, having been amalgamated to form Trinity in 1546. Indeed, the mid-sixteenth century was a time when all of the colleges were threatened by an Act of Parliament of 1544 enabling King Henry VIII to dissolve them as he had dissolved the monasteries; but Henry was persuaded to take a progressive view of the collegiate function, turning it to his own ends, and with his foundation of Trinity the colleges became training-grounds for a wider range of professional and courtly roles, bringing the University into its early-modern phase and paving the way for its present-day situation, as a place where both arts and science subjects are studied, taught, and researched to the highest level by students and academics from all over the world.

Though now only one among more than 80 English universities, Cambridge retains a strong reputation for academic excellence and continues to be placed at or near the top of the government's ratings for quality of teaching and research, receiving one of the highest annual grants from the public purse. One of the oldest traditions of scientific research thrives here, in the laboratories of the New Museums Site, Downing Site and Tennis Court Road, where scientists have worked since the nineteenth century, as well as in modern premises such as those on the West Cambridge and Addenbrooke's Hospital Sites. In recent years, Cambridge has led the way with important cutting-edge work in fields including software engineering, genetics, nanotechnology, stem cell research and cancer research.

The thoroughly co-educational character of the modern University of Cambridge is a relatively recent development. Even though six of the early Cambridge colleges (Clare, Pembroke, Queens', Christ's, St John's, and Sidney Sussex) were founded by women, they remained male institutions for hundreds of years, the colleges only beginning to allow their fellows to marry as late as 1860; and the first women's colleges (Girton and Newnham), although established here in the 1870s, were not fully recognised as part of the University until some 75 years later. In 1881 women were first allowed to sit Cambridge exams, and in 1916, under force of circumstance during the First World War, women were permitted to take medical exams; but they had to wait until 1948 for full admission into degrees and for membership of the University Senate and Regent House (when, to mark the occasion, Queen Elizabeth – later

5 King's College Backs
(photo by Marc Anderson)

the Queen Mother – was presented with an honorary degree in the Senate-House). In 1960 there were still only three female colleges in the University, the first mixing of the sexes within an undergraduate college occurring in 1972 when Churchill, Clare and King's admitted women. Change then followed rapidly, and today there remain only three colleges with a single-sex undergraduate composition (Newnham, New Hall and Lucy Cavendish), all of them for women. The male:female ratio is currently 52%:48% (as 50%:50% for undergraduates and 55%:45% for postgraduates).

Cambridge has one of the most comprehensive systems of academical dress in the world, with distinctive gowns and hoods worn on formal occasions enabling precise identification of a graduate's degree and in many cases of a student's college. Another tradition is that of May Balls, elaborate night-long entertainments organised by many of the colleges to take place – nowadays always in June – after the summer examinations. Visitors interested in traditional regalia should not miss Ryder & Amies, the University outfitters on King's Parade by Great St

6 Academics in formal dress

(from Ackermann's *A History of the University of Cambridge*, 1815: photo courtesy of Cambridge University Library)

Mary's, where the college shields are displayed and where students can buy ties, scarves and blazers in their college colours. Here also in the window the University sports clubs advertise events and display results. The colleges are well provided with sports grounds in outer-lying parts of the city, and University facilities include Fenner's on Gresham Road (cricket, tennis and gym), the athletics track on Wilberforce Road, and the rugby and soccer grounds on Grange Road. Cambridge University was the first institution to draw up rules governing the game which was the forerunner of modern football: these appeared in 1848.

Important complementary functions of the University are governed by its Press Syndicate, which is responsible for the University's printing and publishing house, Cambridge University Press, an international organisation employing 1,850 people; and its Local Examinations Syndicate (Cambridge Assessment), which produces exams that are sat each year by pupils across the world. The University has a Chancellor, currently Prince Philip, the Duke of Edinburgh, who was installed on 10 June 1977 – his fifty-sixth birthday. In 2007, marking his thirtieth year in post, a new Professorship was established: the Prince Philip Chair of Ecology and Evolutionary Biology, supplementing the Prince Philip Chair of Technology established at his twenty-fifth. His predecessors as Chancellor have included Lord Burghley, chief minister to Queen Elizabeth I, and Albert, Prince Consort to Queen Victoria – whose fine

7 Passageway from
Clare Old Court
to Clare Bridge

statue by John Henry Foley is in Wolfson College. The full-time Vice-Chancellor is the administrative head of the University.

The city is also now home to a second university, Anglia Ruskin University, situated on East Road beyond Parker's Piece. Previously Anglia Polytechnic University (from 1992), and before that the Cambridgeshire College of Arts & Technology (from 1960), Anglia Ruskin has its origins partly in the Institute for Technical Education first built in East Road in 1889. It takes its present name, adopted in 1995, from the art critic John Ruskin who opened a school of art in Sidney Street in 1858. 28,000 students are spread mainly between this campus and another at Chelmsford in Essex.

The centre of Cambridge has changed markedly since the first edition of this guidebook was published in 1994. Vehicle access has been restricted due to congestion, and there is sometimes more of a commercial air about the colleges, which make increasing use of their buildings and location to attract summer schools, conferences and other business activities. Many colleges have full-time development directors co-ordinating fundraising campaigns. The student-loan system has taken hold, causing students to carry a burden of debt which colleges and the University attempt to ameliorate through generous bursaries. The University itself is engaged in major fundraising activity, reaching out to its 170,000 alumni around the world with an '800th Anniversary Campaign' designed to raise £1bn by 2012, and in 2007 appointed its first Chief Investment Officer to manage its endowment fund. In the last ten years the University has created 250 new professorships and invested £600m in new and refurbished buildings. The city of Cambridge has seen large-scale residential and retail development within a short train commute of London, the Grand Arcade on St Andrew's Street (2008) providing one example.

Library building has been a noticeable feature of the last couple of decades. Cambridge is truly rich in libraries, with 113 at the last count. At a time when so much appears to be going electronic, it is telling that the University should remain dedicated to providing suitable physical spaces for access to the world's information and for proper storage of its precious books and manuscripts. In the centre of the city, newer highlights are the Jerwood Library of Trinity Hall (1998), Jesus College Quincentenary Library (1996), St John's College Library (1994), and the internal refurbishment of the Cockerell Building to house the collections of Gonville and Caius (1997). Further afield, the University Library has been significantly extended, the Sidgwick Site features splendid new faculty libraries including Sir Norman Foster's spectacular addition to the Faculty of Law (1996), the Chemistry Department on Lensfield Road has a new library, and colleges which have provided new building or expansion or refurbishment of library spaces include Corpus Christi, Girton, Lucy Cavendish, New Hall, Newnham, Pembroke, Peterhouse and Wolfson.

The so-called 'Cambridge Phenomenon', which in the 1980s saw the proliferation of software, pharmaceutical and other high-tech companies capitalizing on research activities within the University, has matured in the form of fully integrated academic-business relationships in evidence on the West Cambridge Site with the William Gates Building and BP Institute standing close to the famous Cavendish Laboratory of Physics.

8 Central Cambridge from the south

(photo courtesy of University of Cambridge Air Photograph Library)

Microsoft, Hitachi, Intel and Sony all have centres in Cambridge, and the Judge Business School offers students a Cambridge M.B.A. at the heart of what it describes as "the most dynamic and successful entrepreneurial cluster in Europe". Cambridge Assessment (exams) and Cambridge University Press (publishing), with combined annual turnover close to £350m, are global enterprises at the cutting-edge of e-pedagogy. The science and business parks developed in the '80s by colleges like Trinity and St John's continue to thrive.

Central Cambridge: A Guide to the University and Colleges joins a long lineage of guidebooks to the city, early examples including Thomas

Salmon's *The Foreigner's Companion through the Universities of Cambridge and Oxford* (1748) and *Cantabrigia Depicta: A Concise and Accurate Description of the University and Town of Cambridge and its Environs* (1763). While focusing principally on the central colleges, *Central Cambridge* also describes many of the important non-collegiate sites to be found here, such as libraries, laboratories, and lecture halls. The University's eight museums receive descriptions: all are open to the public (though weekend opening is limited). Non-University museums in Cambridge include the Folk Museum on Castle Street below Kettle's Yard and the Museum of Technology on Cheddars Lane (one and a half miles north-east along the river).

It is the policy of some Cambridge colleges to charge visitors for entry, or to restrict accessibility in other ways, but this guidebook avoids listing either entry fees or opening hours, since practices change and vary so frequently depending on the season, the college, the purpose of the visit, and other events taking place in the grounds or premises. The three main college attractions are King's, Trinity and St John's, but if in the height of summer these are too crowded or expensive for your taste, you will discover many other attractive sites to visit, all of them with entries in this book. It is to be hoped that the visitor, at no matter what time of year, will find enough of the University easily accessible to gain a lasting impression of its historical richness and beauty, along with a sense of its present importance as a place of learning.

9 University of Cambridge arms, granted in 1573 ("Gules, a cross ermine between four lions passant gardant or, and on the cross a closed book fessways gules clasped and garnished gold, the clasps downward": see also p.109)

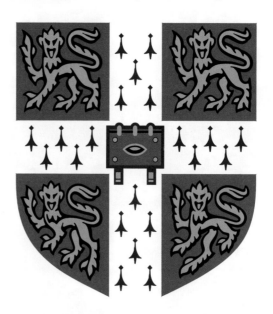

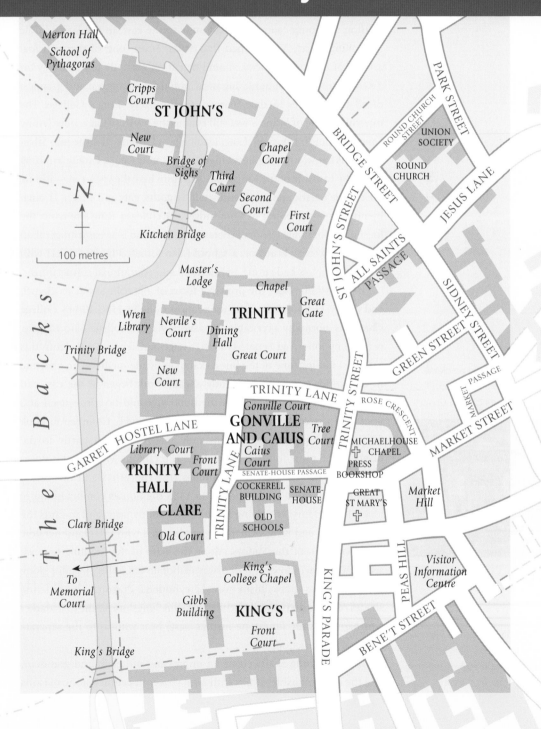

Merton Hall
School of
Pythagoras

Cripps
Court

ST JOHN'S

New
Court

Bridge of
Sighs

Chapel
Court

Third
Court

Second
Court

First
Court

Kitchen Bridge

N

100 metres

The Backs

Master's
Lodge

Chapel

TRINITY

Great
Gate

Wren
Library

Nevile's
Court

Dining
Hall

Great Court

Trinity Bridge

New
Court

TRINITY LANE

Gonville Court

**GONVILLE
AND CAIUS**

Tree
Court

GARRET HOSTEL LANE

Library Court

Front
Court

**TRINITY
HALL**

Caius
Court

SENATE-HOUSE PASSAGE

TRINITY LANE

MICHAELHOUSE
CHAPEL

PRESS
BOOKSHOP

CLARE

COCKERELL
BUILDING

SENATE-
HOUSE

GREAT
ST MARY'S

Market
Hill

Clare Bridge

Old Court

OLD
SCHOOLS

To
Memorial
Court

King's
College Chapel

Gibbs
Building

KING'S

Front
Court

King's Bridge

BRIDGE STREET

ST JOHN'S STREET

ROUND CHURCH STREET

UNION
SOCIETY

ROUND
CHURCH

PARK STREET

JESUS LANE

ALL SAINTS PASSAGE

SIDNEY STREET

GREEN STREET

TRINITY STREET

ROSE CRESCENT

MARKET PASSAGE

MARKET STREET

KING'S PARADE

PEAS HILL

BENE'T STREET

Visitor
Information
Centre

King's College

Both the river and the main streets of Cambridge lie on a north-south axis. The city's main thoroughfare has shifted further eastwards over the years as the University has come to colonise the river banks – until the present day, when the commercial focus of Cambridge for many residents is the Grafton shopping centre, almost a mile to the east. In the later Middle Ages, King Henry VI ordained that Milne Street, one of the principal arteries of the medieval city, should be cut off abruptly to make way for a new river site accommodating what would be the biggest and grandest of all the colleges to date, named appropriately: King's College. The interrupted line of Milne Street still runs to the north (what is now Trinity Lane) and south (Queens' Lane, leading past Queens' College into Silver Street). What was the medieval high street is now King's Parade, running along the east side of the King's site, and from here the visitor may admire the college's elaborate nineteenth-century gothic gate and screen. Though by no means the oldest of Cambridge's 31 colleges, King's remains the focal point for many visitors; it dates from 1441 and is a year younger than Eton College near Windsor, a school (also founded by Henry VI) with which King's has had strong architectural and educational connections.

In the Middle Ages the principal focus of any college was its chapel, and Henry VI himself laid the foundation stone in 1446. King's College Chapel is normally accessible to visitors via the college's north gate, reached by following Senate-House Passage and Trinity Lane. From this gate the building, one of the finest examples of late-medieval architecture in the world, looms magnificently ahead. Work began at the east end (nearest King's Parade), so that the building could be consecrated and used for services even as construction continued. Completion took 80 years, the process being constantly interrupted due partly to the diversion of royal funds into warfare. The famous Wars of the Roses raged in England between two families (the Lancasters and the Yorks) claiming succession to the throne. In 1485 the houses combined under a new king, Henry VII, giving rise to the Tudor dynasty, and towards the later, western end King's Chapel is emblazoned with the grand heraldic ornamentation of the Tudors. Along the sides of the building here we see above the windows and doorway elaborate examples of Tudor stone carving: crowns, portcullises, roses, greyhounds, dragons. The differing shades of stone on the walls (white Yorkshire limestone to the east, darker Northamptonshire limestone further west) bear witness to the separate stages of construction.

Inside, soaring shafts create an impression of height and grandeur, and the craftsmanship of fifteenth- and sixteenth-century stone masons

10 Tudor emblems above west door of King's College Chapel

11 (*Opposite*) Interior of King's College Chapel looking west from high altar

12 Choristers from King's College School cross King's Bridge on their way to the Chapel

is revealed at its best. The carving of the motifs and figures around the walls, the graceful design of the columns, and the intricate fan-vault above our heads (the largest anywhere), all repay close attention. The vault stands 24 metres above the ground, while the chapel extends for 88 metres from end to end, and is 12 metres wide. Above the stone vault (between it and the wooden, lead-capped roof) is a space high enough to walk along. In the windows we see one of the biggest and best collections of sixteenth-century stained glass produced under Flemish inspiration: it depicts, in the upper parts, scenes from the Old Testament and, below them, corresponding New Testament stories. Despite the Biblical subjects, many of the details (costumes, townscapes, a fine Tudor galley) faithfully represent early-Renaissance Europe. During the Second World War this priceless glass was taken out and stored piece by piece, although the chapel thankfully avoided damage, as it had in the English Civil War in spite of a visit in 1643 by one of Cromwell's most notorious despoilers, William Dowsing. The fabulous east window above the altar depicts Christ's crucifixion; while the west window (showing the Last Judgement) is an impressive Victorian addition of 1879.

Half way along, the nave is divided from the chancel by a heavy oak screen bearing sets of initials which include (above the passageway) an intertwined 'H' (for Henry VIII) and 'A' (for Anne Boleyn). The carving can be dated precisely to the early 1530s, for Henry married Anne in 1533 and had her beheaded in 1536. Other carving on the screen (flowers, beasts, heads of cherubs) is of the finest order, almost certainly the work of continental artists brought from France or Italy by Henry

13 King's College Chapel and Gibbs Building from the west
(photo by Marc Anderson)

VIII. Surmounting the screen is the huge organ in its seventeenth-century case, frequently used for services, recitals, and concerts, including the famous Festival of Nine Lessons and Carols on Christmas Eve, broadcast live across the world. King's has a choir of international standing, which consists of 14 adult male choral scholars, and 16 boy choristers aged between nine and fourteen selected from King's College School attached to the college. There is also King's Voices, a mixed-voice choir formed in 1997 to allow women to sing choral music at a high level.

Passing through the interior of the screen we find ourselves in the east end, much of it completed before the arrival of the Tudor kings and therefore plainer and sparser in its ornamentation, with the exception of the fine wooden choir stalls, added in the time of Henry VIII (with canopies dating from 1633). Note also the Swedish candles, made of special wax to prevent smoke from blackening the stonework of the chapel. In front of the stalls stands a bronze lectern of the late fifteenth or early sixteenth century, with a small figure of Henry VI on top.

Behind the altar of King's College Chapel stands Rubens's *Adoration of the Magi* (1633-4), given to the college by a wealthy benefactor, having fetched a record price at auction, and placed here (following a debate about its suitability in this setting) in 1968. Finally, it is worth peering into some of the 18 side chapels containing fan-vaulting and precious glass. Through a door to the north of the chancel an exhibition may be visited, noting at the entrance a sturdy oak wardrobe of c.1480 designed to hold vestments for use in the chapel.

Leaving the chapel and turning to the west, with the great west door (opened for weddings and other ceremonial occasions) behind us, we look across a well-kept lawn to the river, and beyond to rough pasture still grazed by cows, reminding us that nowhere in this East Anglian market town is very far from the country. To the right, the mellow stone of Clare College's Old Court provides a soft contrast with the gothic of King's; and to our left, the stately Gibbs Building of 1724-32 (named after its architect James Gibbs, who also designed the University Senate-House) rises in white Portland stone. Back in Front Court a statue of the founder, Henry VI, perches on top of a fountain, while the Gibbs Building now blocks our view to the river, its elaborately pedimented central arch flanked on each side by eight three-storeyed classical bays creating a strong impression of width. To the east extend the neo-gothic screens bordering King's Parade, and on the south side stands the dining-hall range. The screens and hall imitate the style of the chapel but were in fact designed more than 350 years after it, by William Wilkins in the 1820s. It is well worth walking round Front Court and along the path to the river at King's Bridge, for a fine view back towards the chapel.

The poet Rupert Brooke, who died in the 1914-18 war, lived in King's until 1909 before moving out to his idyllic Grantchester, the village two and a half miles south of Cambridge immortalised in his poem 'The Old Vicarage, Grantchester'. His acquaintances included E. M. Forster (1879-1970), whose novels *The Longest Journey* and *Maurice* draw autobiographically on Cambridge life and who returned to live in King's in his old age, having first entered the college as a student in 1897. Economist John Maynard Keynes was a Fellow of King's from 1924 until his death in 1946 and was the college's bursar. Other fellows have included the pioneer of computer science and artificial intelligence Alan Turing, and more recently sociologist Anthony Giddens who theorised the so-called 'Third Way' in modern British politics.

Despite its grandeur and centrality, King's is not one of the largest undergraduate colleges, with only 380 students at first-degree level. It enjoys a reputation as a relaxed place in which liberal attitudes and a tolerance of informality are combined with high academic standards. Its 200 graduate students (taking a second degree), 110 fellows and 250 non-academic staff bolster its size.

Map E8

Clare College

Founded in 1326 as University Hall and re-founded in 1338 as Clare Hall, this is the second oldest of Cambridge's 31 colleges. Originally fronting the medieval Milne Street (cut off by the building of King's Chapel), Clare's entrance is now tucked away at the end of Trinity Lane near the north gate of King's. The old buildings were slowly demolished in the seventeenth century, making way for one of the neatest and most satisfying of Cambridge's courtyards, built by local architects Thomas Grumbold and his son Robert between 1638 and 1715. The warmth of the yellow stone is best appreciated from the riverbank on King's College Backs, making the outer south side of the court one of the most photographed buildings in England.

Within, the classicism of Old Court is broken by occasional gothic features, including the fan-vaulting in the gateway – one of the last uses in England of a style brought to perfection in King's Chapel more than 100 years earlier. While King's had been delayed by the Wars of the Roses, Clare's reconstruction was interrupted by the English Civil War (1642-9), during which Oliver Cromwell plundered the site for building materials to fortify Cambridge Castle. Clare Chapel, reached in the north-east corner of the court, dates from 1763-9 and was designed by James Burrough (the great amateur architect who was Master of Caius College) and built by James Essex. Its tall wooden lantern illuminating the antechapel is a splendid and unusual feature, particularly from inside.

Clare Hall became Clare College in 1856 (and a new Clare Hall was founded separately as a graduate college in 1966). The name comes from Lady Elizabeth de Clare, a wealthy granddaughter of Edward I who endowed the foundation of 1338. All that remains of the medieval court she paid for is a stone panel with a shield representing the college arms, now above the doorway to the small hall opposite the entrance to the main dining hall accessible via steps in the middle of the north range. Lady Clare was widowed three times and the periphery of her crest features tears as emblems of mourning.

Clare's most pleasing single feature is its bridge spanning the river, reached through the gateway on the west side of the court, but viewed at its best from King's Bridge to the south or Garret Hostel Bridge to the north – or indeed from a punt on the river. Thomas Grumbold erected this in 1638, and it is now the oldest bridge on the Cam. American novelist Henry James, who had an eye for exquisite structures, admired it and described the way that the line of its balustrade can be seen rising and then "gently collapsing" in the central section.

It is worth following Clare Avenue (laid out in 1690) through the iron gates (erected in 1714), past the beautiful Fellows' Gardens with their lily pool enclosed on three sides by a clipped yew hedge (inspired by a garden at Pompeii), and on across Queen's Road to the site of Clare Memorial and Thirkill Courts (1923-55), built to release the college finally from its longstanding confinement within the solitary Old Court. The architect who inaugurated this scheme was Giles Gilbert

14 Clare College from King's Backs

15 Punting on the Cam at Clare Bridge

16 Clare College: the post bike

(photo by Alan McArthur)

Scott, shortly afterwards responsible for the new University Library just to the west. Clare now grew rapidly, the new building work of the 1950s funded largely by American philanthropist Paul Mellon, a member of the college. This site helped to accommodate women undergraduates when Clare opened its doors to them in the autumn of 1972 – the first undergraduate college, along with King's and Churchill, to become co-residential. Memorial Court (to the north) has now been divided into two parts, re-designated Memorial Court and Ashby Court, by the addition of the octagonal Forbes Mellon Library block in 1986. One effect has been to diminish the visual dominance of the University Library over the site. Statues on the Queen's Road side include Henry Moore's *The Falling Warrior* and Charles Jencks' *D.N.A. Double Helix*.

Like many of the ancient colleges in central Cambridge, Clare has another site lying away from the centre. This is known as The Colony and is situated near the corner of Castle Street and Chesterton Lane behind St Giles's Church, on land that has been in Clare's ownership for hundreds of years and which now houses more than half of the college's undergraduates.

Clare's former members include Hugh Latimer, the Protestant reformer burned at the stake by Mary I in 1555, and Nicholas Ferrar, founder in 1625 of the Anglican community at Little Gidding (subject of one of T. S. Eliot's poems *Four Quartets*). Ferrar was a fervent supporter of colonial expansion in Virginia, and Clare retained strong connections with the New World, offering places throughout the eighteenth century to the sons of eminent American families. Archbishop of Canterbury Rowan Williams was formerly Dean of Clare. Naturalist David Attenborough read Natural Sciences here and writer Peter Ackroyd read English.

Clare holds the record for the longest-serving Master: Dr Edward Atkinson occupied the Master's lodge here for an extraordinary 59 years from 1856 to 1915.

Map E7

Trinity Hall

Traditionally a college strong in the study of Law, and with a reputation for the quality of its kitchens, Trinity Hall lies due north of Clare. It is quite distinct from Trinity College, which it pre-dates by some 200 years, but whose existence prevented it from following the nineteenth-century trend of changing its name from 'Hall' to 'College'. This is the only ancient Cambridge college still to be known as a Hall.

William Bateman, Bishop of Norwich, who was to oversee the early years of neighbouring Gonville Hall after the death of Edmund Gonville, decided in 1350 to found his own college devoted to Law. Although this emphasis changed in the mid-nineteenth century, Trinity Hall retains a reputation for legal studies, producing a fine array of judges, barristers, and lawyers. Among its most famous products (and certainly the most powerful) was Stephen Gardiner (1497-1555), who was Master of Trinity Hall as well as Chancellor of the University, Bishop of Winchester, Lord Chancellor of England, chief advisor to Henry VIII and Mary I, and said by some to be the English Machiavelli. A later fellow of the college was Leslie Stephen, editor of the *Dictionary of National Biography*, whose daughter Virginia met her future husband Leonard Woolf in Cambridge. Virginia Woolf evokes the city and University in her *Jacob's Room* (1922) and *A Room of One's Own* (1929), the latter of which was derived from lectures she delivered in Cambridge. Modern alumni of Trinity Hall include writer J. B. Priestley, National Theatre director Nicholas Hytner, and broadcaster Andrew Marr.

At the bend in Trinity Lane, close to where Trinity Hall joins Clare, the visitor will notice collars of metal spikes around the drainpipe running past the first-floor rooms: a measure to prevent students climbing into their lodgings late at night after the porters' lodge has closed. 'Night climbing' was once a favourite (if illicit) pursuit among students, who have been known to scale the heights of King's College Chapel to suspend items – including a line of washing and a 'Ban the Bomb' banner – between the pinnacles. Once an Austin 7 car was hauled by night onto the roof of the Senate-House. Whipplesnaith's book

17 Bishop William Bateman, founder of Trinity Hall

(from Ackermann's *A History of the University of Cambridge*, 1815: photo courtesy of Cambridge University Library)

The Night Climbers of Cambridge (1937; re-issued 2007) remains the classic account of this activity (see photo on p.37).

Trinity Hall's Front Court (beyond the porters' lodge) dates from the period after the foundation of 1350 but was ashlar-faced and otherwise converted in more recent times, visible evidence of the fourteenth century being limited to an exposed two-light gothic window on the first floor in the north-west corner, sunk behind the later additions, and (through a passage in the north wall) the outer face of the range, on which the original clunch fabric is almost totally revealed. These elements show the layered effect typical of many college buildings in Cambridge, with alterations and restorations compounding earlier work.

A quiet chapel, probably begun in 1352 (making it the earliest of the college chapels – it is also one of the smallest) is entered in the south-west corner of Front Court. In the antechapel two windows commemorate

18 Trinity Hall's Jerwood Library next to Garret Hostel Bridge.

19 Trinity Hall's crest: the arms of the See of Norwich impaling those of Bishop Bateman (photo by D. A. Thomas)

the elevation of Robert Runcie, formerly Dean of Trinity Hall, to the Archbishopric of Canterbury (1980). The college crest displayed prominently on the painted roof of the chapel and on the pediments and wall of the court features a gorget (a crescent-shaped piece of armour worn around the throat), often coupled with Bishop Bateman's mitres. On the north side of the court the crest appears above a numbered plaque: this is the college's insurance number, identifying it in case of fire and dating from the days when the fire brigades were controlled by insurance companies with their own symbols – in this case a sun.

An archway beneath the western pediment leads to Library Court, where we find one of central Cambridge's architectural delights: the combination of the old library with its 'chained' books (c.1580), in Elizabethan red brick with a stepped gable at the far end, and its recent echo in the Jerwood Library (1998) overhanging the river. Here seats overlook Garret Hostel Bridge, while the Fellows' Garden lies over the wall to the south. Author Henry James wrote in 1883 that "If I were called upon to mention the prettiest corner of the world, I should draw a thoughtful sigh and point the way to the garden of Trinity Hall." Unlike most other Backs colleges, Trinity Hall stops here and does not own land on the western riverbank.

Expansion at Trinity Hall is limited by its position, but the small site has been skilfully developed, with unobtrusive modern extensions along the Garret Hostel Lane edge culminating in the splendid new library. In 1948 the college purchased Wychfield, a bigger site between Huntingdon Road and Storey's Way, which in recent years has spawned the largest development of new college accommodation anywhere in Cambridge.

Old Schools

Map E8

20 Old Schools gatehouse, Trinity Lane

On Trinity Lane, almost opposite the entrance to Clare, stands a gateway leading to the administrative core of the University of Cambridge: the Old Schools. This site is also the historical centre of the University, for it incorporates buildings begun in about 1350 and in use as lecture rooms by 1400, representing the earliest surviving attempt to provide a central forum where students and scholars from all of the colleges, halls and hostels that were springing up around Cambridge could come together for a common education. The gatehouse dates from 1441 and was until 1829 part of King's College, but it remained incomplete for 400 years, the lower half being restored and the upper half built anew (1864-7) by George Gilbert Scott. The Old Schools site is the first of many in Cambridge which belong not to any particular college but to the University itself.

21 End of Trinity Lane showing medieval gatehouse (now part of the Old Schools) before Scott's renovation, with King's College Chapel beyond

(from Harraden's *Illustrations of the University of Cambridge*, 1830: photo courtesy of Cambridge University Library)

22 Across Caius Court, Gonville and Caius College, to Senate-House Passage with the Gate of Honour at centre

(from Harraden's *Cantabrigia Depicta: A Series of Engravings*, 1809-11: photo courtesy of Cambridge University Library)

Half way up nearby Senate-House Passage, a gap with steps affords a view of the arcaded eighteenth-century façade of the Old Schools (1754-8), behind which can just be seen a portion of the old rubble wall of the lecture rooms completed by 1400, including a gothic window. This, the range containing the original Divinity School, is the oldest building to survive from the early public University (though some of the colleges feature earlier work). The various buildings around the Old Schools yards nowadays house offices and formal rooms, including the University Combination Room, the University Registry, and the Council Room: these are not open to visitors.

Map E7

Cockerell Building

The word BIBLIOTHECA (Latin for LIBRARY) is inscribed appropriately above the doorway of the large structure which flanks the south-western side of Senate-House Passage and towers in the foreground above the Old Schools. This is the Cockerell Building (1837-42), the work of Victorian architect C. R. Cockerell, constructed to house the rapidly expanding University Library which had previously been contained within the neighbouring Old Schools precincts since 1438. The main University book collections moved to their present site in west Cambridge in 1934 and the roomy Cockerell Building was subsequently host to the library of the History Faculty until it moved to the Sidgwick Site in the 1960s, and then to that of the Law Faculty until the mid 1990s. In 1992 adjacent Gonville and Caius College, which has housed its books and manuscripts in a library since 1441, purchased a 350-year lease on the building from the University and turned it into the most spacious and atmospheric of college libraries, officially opened in 1997.

Map F7

Senate-House

The Senate-House is the ceremonial centre of Cambridge, where degrees are conferred on students and distinguished visitors, where formal votes are taken on decisions affecting the life of the University, and where important public lectures are delivered. Here undergraduates first discover their examination results, listed on special boards placed along the south wall, at the end of the academic year in May and June; here too students from each college process in their academic gowns to receive a piece of paper certifying them as graduates of the University of Cambridge, in a special ceremony during which the Vice-Chancellor of the University or a deputy makes an official pronouncement in Latin.

23 Graduation day on Senate-House lawn

The 'Senate' is the collective name given to all holders of Cambridge degrees at M.A. level or higher. The Senate is represented for practical purposes by the 'Regent House', whose membership is invited to the Senate-House building when contentious issues relating to the legislation, constitution, and actions of the University need to be voted upon. Thus, the Senate-House is, both symbolically and actually, the very hub of the University of Cambridge, where important administrative and academic policies are determined and decisions taken with appropriate formal aplomb.

The building itself is, in some ways even more than King's Chapel, the architectural centrepiece of Cambridge. Built 1722-30 in a restrained baroque style by James Gibbs, with the help of James Burrough, its well-proportioned windows, pediments, parapet, and Corinthinan pilasters and columns present a stately effect rising from the neat lawn with its central urn and its black railings of 1730 (among the first to be put up in England). Inside, an ante-room leads into a spacious hall with galleries on either side.

The Senate-House had been intended by Gibbs as part of a three-sided court of buildings, but this, like Cockerell's later scheme to cover the site of the Old Schools with Victorian structures, and Nicholas Hawksmoor's earlier one to convert the centre of Cambridge into a grand classical forum, never came about. Additions subsequent to the Senate-House were limited to Stephen Wright's east-facing façade of the Old Schools and Cockerell's University Library. The view across the whole site from King's Parade, with the railings and lawn in the foreground, is the most stately in Cambridge. The urn on its plinth is a bronze copy, donated to the University in 1842, of the Warwick Vase, a Roman urn from the second century AD now in Glasgow's Burrell Collection. The Senate-House stands to the north, while Wright's well-matched Old Schools façade forms a western border, the high windows, cornice, and parapet of its upper section rising above a five-arched open undercroft. Meanwhile the gothic grandeur of King's College Chapel looms behind a massive horse-chestnut tree on its lawn to the south.

Map F7

Cambridge University Press Bookshop

On the corner opposite the Senate-House lies the oldest bookshop site in England, where books have been sold since at least 1581. Former occupants have included the Macmillan brothers, Alexander and Daniel, who set up here in 1845 before moving to London to make their fortune as publishers. Since 1992 the building has been the bookshop and showroom of the oldest printer and publisher in the world, the

24 Cambridge
University Press
bookshop with
Senate-House behind
(photo by The
Photographic Unit)

University's own press, Cambridge University Press, which began printing books on a site near here (where the Senate-House lawn now lies) in 1584, the University having received from Henry VIII in 1534 a royal charter permitting it to print. In 2009 the Press celebrates its 425th anniversary of continuous production, but it also has one of the largest current outputs of any international educational or academic publisher, and here the entire range of its list, covering all levels from primary English learning materials through to the most specialised research, is accessible. The Press's academic list features 52 Nobel Prize winners.

This bookshop, along with the Pitt Building on Trumpington Street (see pp.49-50), represents the Press in central Cambridge; but the publishing and printing operations are now based a mile and a half to the south on Shaftesbury Road (see p.105), while branches in New York, Melbourne, Madrid, Singapore, Cape Town, São Paolo, New Delhi and Dubai, and many offices and representatives in other parts of the world, continue to expand the business abroad. The Press's publications have included the Geneva Bible (1591), Milton's *Lycidas* (1638), the *Book of Common Prayer* (1638), Newton's *Principia Mathematica* (second ed., 1713), G. E. Moore's *Principia Ethica* (1903), and the New English Bible (1961-70). In 1877 the Press Syndicate turned down what later became the *Oxford English Dictionary*, thereby contributing to the eventual fortunes of its great rival.

A wall-chart shows the history of the Press, and on the wall of the first floor is a framed letter of 18 January 1947 from Albert Einstein, enquiring about his royalties.

27

Map F8

Great St Mary's (the University Church)

Although overshadowed in grandeur by King's College Chapel across the road, the Church of St Mary the Great is an important late-gothic building begun in 1478 and lying at the very heart of Cambridge. An

25 Great St Mary's: across the market place; and interior looking west towards the University organ

26 Great St Mary's tower

earlier church had existed on the same site since at least 1205 and probably much earlier, and it is likely that the medieval Old Schools were deliberately placed in the vicinity of this focal point. Certainly by 1478 the scholars were ready to build here a special 'University Church'; and until the Senate-House was built 250 years later, University degree ceremonies were held inside Great St Mary's. Sermons are still preached to the University by visiting speakers on Sunday evenings during term from the pulpit, which can be moved along on rails; and although it is an Anglican parish church, Great St Mary's also receives a special financial contribution towards its regular running and maintenance costs from the University.

The top of the church tower, completed in 1608 and reached by 123 spiral steps, offers the best of all views of the surrounding colleges. From this tower were first heard the 'Westminster' chimes familiar today as those rung by Big Ben in London, and also now heard from Sydney and Adelaide town halls in Australia, rung in the bell towers of various American universities, and frequently broadcast before the time-signal on British radio programmes – they were designed for Great St Mary's by Dr Joseph Jowett of Trinity Hall in 1793. A curfew calling students back to their colleges was rung from the tower at nine in the evening for several hundred years, until 1939.

The church's high aisle arches and spacious clerestory windows are light and elegant, offset by the dark timber of the roof (donated in 1505 by Henry VII in the form of 100 oaks) and pews. Tiered galleries in the aisles date from the eighteenth century, when the seating capacity was increased to 1,700, and in this period the building was considered roomy enough to house a fire engine at one end. While King's College Chapel marks an important national development in architectural history, St Mary the Great belongs to the great East Anglian tradition of church building of the late fifteenth century, and can be viewed in the context of other regional masterpieces on a similar scale, such as the churches at Lavenham and Saffron Walden. A typically East Anglian feature is the poppy-head carving at the ends of the pews.

Outside, a circular mark on the south-west buttress of the tower is the official centre-point of Cambridge from which distances were first measured in 1725 by a series of milestones, said to be the first in Britain since Roman times. Many of them still exist along the roads towards London, Huntingdon and Essex.

In 2002 a place-finder model of central Cambridge, complete with names in Braille, was erected near the church alongside seats proclaiming this 'Senate House Hill'. Until 1767 shops abutted the west wall of Great St Mary's here, crowding into King's Parade.

29

Gonville and Caius College

Gonville and Caius (usually abbreviated to Caius, pronounced 'Keys') is the fourth oldest of the colleges. The only college in Cambridge or Oxford to include the names of two founders in its title, it occupies a central position, both geographically and, with a student population of some 750 and significant wealth, in the life of the University.

Founded in 1348 (the year in which the Black Death broke out in England) by a Norfolk priest called Edmund Gonville, the original Gonville Hall provided premises in Cambridge for trainee priests supported largely by money raised from tenants on church estates in rural Norfolk – money which was to sustain the college for the next 200 years. Gonville's aim was to send men educated here back into the locality to serve as clergy and scholars. He died in 1351 and work on his college was continued by Bishop William Bateman, who had founded neighbouring Trinity Hall in 1350.

The 1390s saw the completion of the chapel, reached via Tree Court (with its lovely avenue of whitebeams unusual among Cambridge's normally treeless inner courts) and Caius Court. Inside the chapel visitors may pull back a hinged wooden panel beneath the kneeling tomb-figure of Master and benefactor Thomas Legge on the right-hand side to reveal a section of the late fourteenth-century wall still standing beneath more recent embellishments. Also of note in the chapel are the splendid alabaster tomb of the second founder, John Caius, with its classical columns and surmounting skull; the golden cherubs adorning the ceiling; and the imposing organ installed in 1981.

A right turn outside the chapel leads to Gonville Court, the core of the original college of 1348, faced with ashlar in the eighteenth century and now splendidly adorned with window boxes and planted borders.

Gonville Hall was enlarged and transformed by John Keys, an eminent physician who had studied in Italy, immersing himself in the humanist learning of the Renaissance and Latinising his name to Caius. The new College of Gonville and Caius, endowed with Dr Caius' money, received its charter from Mary I in 1557. Caius brought a new spirit to Cambridge, rejecting the medievalism of castellated gatehouses and enclosed courtyards (as at Queens' and St John's) and commissioning the construction of a three-sided court, Caius Court, on the Italian model (the fourth side left open to allow air to circulate) and of three stone gates in an eclectic classical style representing Humility, Virtue, and Honour, with Latin inscriptions of these attributes above each gate. This scheme led the student both symbolically and literally from a Humble entrance ('Humilitas' – where the porters' lodge now stands on Trinity Street),

27 Statues of John Caius and William Bateman on the south front of Waterhouse Building, Gonville and Caius College

to a Virtuous daily passage within the college ('Virtutis' – between Tree and Caius Courts), and finally to an Honourable procession under the triumphal arch ('Honoris' – on the open south side of Caius Court) when he graduated. On the Gate of Virtue may be seen the date of construction, 1567; and through the Gate of Honour graduating Caians still process each summer on their way to collect their degrees from the adjacent Senate-House.

Other notable 'Caians' have included William Harvey, who discovered the circulation of the blood; Titus Oates, who hatched the infamous Popish Plot alleging a Catholic conspiracy to kill King Charles II; Edward Wilson, doctor to Captain Scott's ill-fated Antarctic expedition, who flew the college flag at the South Pole in 1912 and died nearby; physiologist Charles Sherrington; James Chadwick, the nuclear physicist who discovered the neutron; political philosopher Michael Oakeshott; Francis Crick, co-discover of the structure of D.N.A.; Joseph Needham, the great historian of Chinese science and civilisation; Stephen Hawking, physicist and best-selling author of *A Brief History of Time*; J. H. Prynne, pre-eminent contemporary British poet; and political figures Kenneth Clarke and Alastair Campbell. Caius is the University's fourth largest college for undergraduates, with nearly 550.

Leaving the college and standing on the cobbles at the head of Senate-House Passage, beneath the turreted Victorian tower with its statues of Caius, Gonville (below), and Bishop Bateman, we may look up at the infamous 'Senate-House Leap', a gap of some two and a half metres between a small turret window and the ledge of the Senate-House roof. A custom (no longer practised) once dared Caius undergraduates to jump across this gap and – more difficult – back again.

Caius was the first college to abolish celibacy among its fellows, in

1860. It admitted women as undergraduates in 1979. Recent expansion includes a lease on the Cockerell Building on Senate-House Passage, to house the college library containing 900 medieval manuscripts and many early printed books in their custom-made seventeenth-century bookcases; and the Stephen Hawking Building (2006) across the river on West Road, where the college already owned the residences Harvey Court and Finella. In 2006 Stephen Hawking also earned the Copley Medal for outstanding achievements in scientific research, the Royal Society's oldest and most prestigious award. Hawking, whose physical capabilites have deteriorated over the years as a result of a degenerative motor neurone disease, is Lucasian Professor of Mathematics in the University (a chair once held by Newton) and is famous for his work linking gravity with quantum theory and solving the qualitative problems in general relativity through an investigation of space-time structure, black holes and the Big Bang.

Map F7   Michaelhouse Chapel

St Michael's, on the east side of Trinity Street, once doubled as a college chapel and a parish church. It served two colleges: Michaelhouse, a foundation of 1324 absorbed into Trinity College in 1546; and Gonville and Caius, in its early incarnation as Gonville Hall. The architecture (1324-50) is of the decorated gothic period, with characteristic reticulated tracery in the windows. The building is now known as Michaelhouse Chapel or the Michaelhouse Centre or just Michaelhouse, doubling as a place of worship and a cafeteria, art gallery and concert venue. The chancel contains a reredos of the Last Supper by Giles Gilbert Scott, and a quiet smaller chapel through a door to the south is named after Hervey de Stanton, Chief Justice of England, Chancellor of the Exchequer to Edward II, and founder of Michaelhouse. Behind the church stands St Michael's Court (1903), belonging to Gonville and Caius.

Map F6   Trinity College

A tour of the largest and wealthiest of the colleges, Trinity, is best begun on the cobbles outside the Great Gate on Trinity Street. Generations of renowned thinkers have passed through this gatehouse, for Trinity College's list of alumni reads like a *Who's Who* of British intellectual and literary history. Members of Trinity have included Francis Bacon and Isaac Newton; the philosophers G. E. Moore, Bertrand Russell and Ludwig Wittgenstein; historians Thomas Babington Macaulay and his great-nephew George Macaulay Trevelyan; anthropologist J. G. Frazer;

physicist James Clerk Maxwell; mathematicians A. N. Whitehead, G. H. Hardy and J. E. Littlewood; astrophysicist A. S. Eddington; poets George Herbert, Andrew Marvell, John Dryden, Lord Byron, Alfred Tennyson, A. E. Housman and Thom Gunn; and writers William Thackeray, A. A. Milne and Vladimir Nabokov. The best-known undergraduate in modern times was Prince Charles, who came up in 1967 and graduated with a degree in History and Archaeology in 1970; his grandfather King George VI and great-great grandfather Edward VII also studied here. Trinity College has produced 31 Nobel Prize winners, beginning in the early twentieth century with the outstanding physicists Lord Rayleigh (1904), J. J. Thomson (1906), Ernest Rutherford (1908) and William Bragg (1915). In the 1820s and '30s Trinity helped spawn the Cambridge Apostles, a discussion group which was to play a part in forming the minds of many leading members of the British intelligentsia, including the infamous spies Guy Burgess and Anthony Blunt. The first Prime Minister of India, Jawaharlal Nehru, read Natural Sciences here.

Trinity was founded in 1546 by King Henry VIII, whose statue stands over the Great Gate. The king holds in his left hand a golden orb surmounted by a cross representing universal Christianity, and in his right a royal sceptre; but the latter symbol has been replaced by something more mundane: a chair leg standing in for the original which student pranksters have removed. Beneath Henry we see the royal coat-of-arms representing Edward III, founder of an earlier college on this site, King's Hall. Edward, king of England during the Black Death and Hundred Years' War, also

28 Trinity Great Court, with the fountain and Great Gate

29 Edward III and Henry VIII (statue) commemorated on Trinity College Great Gate

laid claim to France, and was the first English king to quarter the rampant lions with the French fleur-de-lys, producing the now-familiar arms. Aligned beneath are the shields of his six sons, including the Black Prince (the first Prince of Wales, whose white feathers and motto are still used by Prince Charles today) and a blank white shield (a symbolic heraldic device showing that the bearer – here the young Earl of Hatfield – died in infancy).

The Great Gate was begun in 1518 as the entrance to King's Hall, its size and fortified grandeur – of a kind normally reserved for castles or important manor houses – bearing witness to the esteem in which the Cambridge colleges were held in the later Middle Ages. Henry VIII incorporated King's Hall, along with another old college on the site, Michaelhouse, into the new Trinity in 1546. On the grass near the gate stands an apple tree planted in 1954 and descended from one in the garden of Isaac Newton's home, Woolsthorpe Manor in Lincolnshire. It commemorates the falling apple which is said to have inspired Newton's theory of gravity. The great scientist lived in rooms just north of the Great Gate between 1679 and 1696, and worked here on his *Principia Mathematica*.

Passing through the gate, we enter the largest enclosed courtyard in Europe. Trinity Great Court, with a circumference of 370 metres, is the site of a foot race celebrated in the film *Chariots of Fire*. Here athletes attempt to run round the perimeter path before the clock on the tower beside the chapel has struck 24 times, which it does at midday and midnight, taking 45 seconds. The race was staged in 1988 between two top runners, Sebastian Coe and Steve Cram, who barely managed to achieve the feat first recorded by Olympic hurdler Lord Burghley back in 1927.

The court contains all the features typical of Cambridge college architecture. On either side of the Great Gate (with its west-facing statues of James I with his wife Anne of Denmark and son Charles) run ranges of rooms occupied by students and fellows. To the north the chapel, begun in 1555 during the reign of Queen Mary I, presents its gothic windows and pinnacles: inside, the visitor may seek out statues of Bacon, Newton (by Roubiliac), Macaulay and Tennyson, and gaze from the antechapel into the interior with its splendid roof, stalls and reredos. Next to the chapel stands another gatehouse, the earliest in Cambridge, built originally 1427-37 for King's Hall; and on the west range lies the creeper-clad Master's lodge. Trinity's Master is not elected by the fellows but appointed by the Crown. As a political appointment, the Mastership of Trinity might fall to a retiring public figure, as in the case of R. A. Butler, a former Chancellor of the Exchequer, who occupied this lodge in the 1960s. A new Master arriving at Trinity must knock ceremonially on the doors of the Great Gate before gaining admittance.

30 Trinity's Wren Library: interior; and from the Backs

The court has an elegant central fountain (1601-15; rebuilt 1715), whose water comes from an underground conduit one and a half miles long, first constructed in the fourteenth century by Franciscan friars to serve their monastery where Sidney Sussex College now stands; and yet another gatehouse on the south range, featuring a statue of Queen Elizabeth I, daughter of the founder. South of the Master's lodge stands the Jacobean dining hall (1604-5), with interior minstrels' gallery, hammerbeam roof and portrait of Henry VIII above the High Table. The glass lantern on top is a particularly attractive feature. A passage, flanked by an oak screen rich in strap-panelling, divides the hall and kitchens. The dessert dish 'crème brûlée' is, despite its French name, said to have been invented in these kitchens.

Beyond the hall to the west lies Nevile's Court, named after Dr Thomas Nevile, Master of Trinity from 1593 to 1615, who sponsored a massive programme of building and expansion. This court has the air of a spacious Roman bathhouse with its high colonnades and classical facades. Here the poet Lord Byron lived, in a suite of rooms on the first floor of the north side, during his time at Trinity (1805-7).

Originally three-sided, Nevile's Court was prolonged and closed at its west end in 1676-95 by the Wren Library, named after its designer, the great architect Christopher Wren. It is his finest architectural achievement outside London. Classical figures, representing (from left to right) Divinity, Law, Physic (i.e. Medicine), and Mathematics, surmount the library, which rests at first-floor level on a row of Tuscan columns in front of grilled openings with views through to the river. The library interior offers an immediate sense of spaciousness, since the floor is sunk deeper and the windows raised higher than has appeared

35

from outside – a trick of perspective by this technically most ingenious of architects. Wren designed the bookcases, which feature superb wood carving by Grinling Gibbons. A number of marble busts sit at the ends of the bookcase cubicles, including one of Newton by Roubiliac (1751); and a life-size statue of Byron (1831) by Danish sculptor Bertil Thorwaldsen should also be noted. Treasures in the library range from an eighth-century copy of the Epistles of St Paul to the original manuscript of *Winnie-the-Pooh*.

On the east side of Nevile's Court, we see Wren's Tribune, the classical platform and staircase built against the west side of the dining hall; and through the southern arches New Court, designed in 1821 by William Wilkins. New Court's western gatehouse leads to the Backs, where excellent views of the library (the peach-coloured hues of its Ketton stone catching the light) and of the lawns stretching north towards St John's can be obtained from Trinity Bridge.

A tour of Trinity is best concluded back near the Great Gate on Trinity Street, where the range opposite is Whewell's Court, named after William Whewell, Master from 1841 to 1866, who helped introduce the study of Natural Sciences at Cambridge. Although Homerton is now slightly larger if postgraduate students are included in the count, Trinity remains the largest college at undergraduate level (with around 750) and has extensive holdings of property in Cambridge and elsewhere. It uses its considerable resources to provide numerous scholarships and grants in the service of higher education, as well as for the support of some of the other colleges.

Map F6

St John's College

St John's is entered from St John's Street through the most colourful of Cambridge gatehouses, its orange bricks framing the carved heraldic arms of Lady Margaret Beaufort (mother of Henry VII), the college's foundress. It is worth pausing on the opposite side of the street to examine the carving, painted to reflect as accurately as possible the original colour-scheme, which features two mythological beasts with surreally horned heads, antelopes' bodies, and the tails of elephants or lions, supporting the royal crest and crown, and flanked by the distinctive portcullises of the Tudor dynasty descended from Lady Margaret. These strange conglomerate animals known as 'yales' are also the symbol of the northern lordship of Kendal, which was one of Margaret's many estates: they stand in a field of coloured flowers which include marguerite daisies, a pun on the name of the foundress. The gatehouse was built at the foundation of the college in 1511. Margaret's

31 New Court, St John's, across the lawns

32 A student 'night climber' atop New Court pinnacles in the 1930s

(from Whipplesnaith's *The Night Climbers of Cambridge*, 1937; re-issued 2007: photo courtesy of Oleander Press)

legacy to Cambridge also included Christ's College, whose gatehouse sports an almost identical coat-of-arms. A devout woman, she promoted the study of divinity: her confessor was John Fisher, Bishop of Rochester and one of her executors, who supervised the foundation of St John's after her death in 1509. The college competes in rowing events under the name 'The Lady Margaret Boat Club' rather than St John's, owing to an incident in which the St John's crew was banned from the river.

On this site in the early Middle Ages stood a hospital named after St John the Evangelist, who was adopted as the new college's patron. A statue of him holding a poisoned chalice (with the head of a serpent – into which St John is said to have converted the poison – emerging over the rim) stands in the canopied niche above the Tudor arms. His and the college's symbol, an eagle, stands near his feet.

Through the gate we enter First Court, once a four-sided yard closed to the north by the old hospital and college chapel, whose foundations are still marked on the lawn. Older buildings remain on three sides, but the fourth was opened up in the 1860s to make room for a massive new chapel in monumental Victorian gothic by the celebrated architect George Gilbert Scott. The pinnacled tower dominates not only this corner of the college, but the whole of the north end of the city centre, and is a prominent landmark from afar. Lifelike statues of notable former members of St John's ('Johnians') stand in niches around the outer wall. A dining hall with two bay windows adjoins the chapel, the window nearest the chapel porch being a Victorian addition replicating the Tudor one further south.

37

33 St John the Evangelist on the gatehouse of St John's College

(photo by Martin Walters)

34 St John's Chapel across Second Court

In medieval manor houses the bay window was aligned with the High Table to illuminate the dais where the nobles sat, and here the southerly window marks the end of the original hall while the northerly one lets light on to the present High Table at the end of the nineteenth-century extension. Students eating here in the early years could be confined to a diet of bread and water as a punishment for petty offences within the college, which included speaking English rather than one of the classical languages they were studying, or wearing their hair too long. More serious crimes listed in the original college statutes include "Theft, murder, incest, notorious adultery or fornication, scaling the walls or opening the gate at night ... to be punished with expulsion"!

An archway beneath a figure of Lady Margaret Beaufort separates the hall from the kitchens, and high up in the south-western corner of First Court on what is now 'F' staircase the poet William Wordsworth discovered his "nook obscure" when he came to live in St John's as a student in 1787:

> Right underneath, the College kitchens made
> A humming sound, less tuneable than bees,
> But hardly less industrious.
>
> *(The Prelude, Book III)*

Another famous W.W., the anti-slavery campaigner William Wilberforce, and his colleague in that noble cause Thomas Clarkson, were near-contemporaries of Wordsworth's at St John's. Thomas Wyatt, who introduced the sonnet into English poetry and was suspected of

35 Bridge of Sighs,
St John's College

an affair with Anne Boleyn, was at John's, as were William Cecil (first Lord Burghley) and his son Robert (first Earl of Salisbury). John Dee, astrologer and occultist, graduated from the college in 1545, and William Gilbert, discoverer of the Earth's magnetism, in 1561. More recent Johnians have included Nobel Prize-winning physicist Paul Dirac (his medal is in the library) and chemist Fred Sanger, and the first Sikh Prime Minister of India, Manmohan Singh.

Inside the chapel, the dark woodwork, deeply coloured glass, and eastern apse have a heavy grandeur characteristic of mid-nineteenth-century church building. Here the chapel choir – standing with that of King's in world renown – sings, its 16 treble boy choristers drawn from St John's College School, an establishment across the river founded for this purpose. The north-western chapel exit leads through Chapel Court, with a library extension of the mid-1990s adding two new wings which match the nearby red-brick range of Second Court, 400 years its senior. Over an arch between Chapel Court and North Court we find the arms, designed and carved by Eric Gill, of John Fisher – whose punning name-emblem or 'rebus' features a fish and an ear (of wheat).

Now we enter Second Court, where on the north side a bay window fronts the first-floor Long Gallery, a room in which the marriage contract between the future King Charles I of England and Henrietta Maria of France is said to have been signed, and in which some of the D-Day landings during the Second World War were planned. One then passes through the Shrewsbury Tower (1598-1602), with a statue of the Countess of Shrewsbury who paid in part for Second Court's construction but failed to meet the full amount of £3,400 she had promised, into the smaller Third Court (1669-72). Built over a period of 150 years and maintaining the use of red brick and cobbles, the three-court scheme gave St John's a sense of architectural unity lacking in other colleges, and also provided plentiful living space for students. St John's for a long time vied with Trinity for the title of 'largest college', and with nearly 600 undergraduates is the second largest in the University at that level.

A left turn across the cobbles of Third Court takes us round a corner and on to the early-eighteenth-century Kitchen Bridge, from which a new vista opens across the lawns and down-river to the much-photographed Bridge of Sighs (1831), named after the even more famous structure in Venice. Cambridge's Bridge of Sighs, which Queen Victoria described in her diary as the most "pretty and picturesque" feature of the University, symbolises a new spirit of expansion, connecting the old part of St John's College with the first development to take place on the marshy west side of the river south of Magdalene Street. Until the 1820s, the Cam provided

39

36 School of Pythagoras, St John's College

a natural western boundary for the University, separating it from the meadows beyond; but faced with demands for extra accommodation St John's took a step across the river and commissioned the extensive neo-gothic New Court (1825-31). The buildings, with their elaborate central lantern known as The Wedding-Cake and covered walkway evoking the ancient university streets of Padua or Bologna, paved the way for further expansion westward. To our right the old brick ranges (with dates of construction, 1624 and 1671, on their gables) dip into the waters of the river in a manner reminiscent of Bruges or Venice, while to our left a route through the cloisters of New Court arrives at the modernist Cripps Building of 1963-7. This extensive residential complex leads at its far north-western end to the so-called School of Pythagoras, a late twelfth-century stone building on two storeys with Norman arches which has no connection with the ancient Greek mathematician but which is said to be one of the oldest surviving houses in England. A sizeable dwelling in Norman terms, it is now used for drama, concerts, and other events. This and the neighbouring Merton Hall, a timber-framed range dating from Tudor times, are owned by St John's.

Tracking back to St John's Street, we find opposite St John's the site (until 1865) of the medieval Church of All Saints; and next to it the neo-gothic former Selwyn Divinity School of 1878-9, built by Basil Champneys in red brick with stone dressing. This was founded by and named after the Lady Margaret Professor of Divinity William Selwyn (brother of Johnian G. A. Selwyn after whom Selwyn College is named). The original Divinity School of c.1400 (now part of the Old Schools) was the centre of the University; and the central location of this successor indicated the ongoing importance of the study of theology and related subjects at Cambridge. In 2000 the Faculty of Divinity moved to another purpose-built location on the Sidgwick Site, following which St John's is now developing the whole triangular area bounded by Bridge Street, St John's Street and All Saints Passage for a mixture of college accommodation and commercial purposes.

Map F6

Round Church (Holy Sepulchre)

Opposite the northern end of St John's Street we find one of only about 11 early round churches surviving in England (though there are records of 23), and one of only four still in use. The shape dates back to the time of the first Christians, who built circular structures around sepulchres or tombs as a symbolic way of protecting and highlighting their contents. In Jerusalem the rotunda of the Church of the Holy Sepulchre of Christ was seen by crusading knights who made their way from Norman

37 Round Church

Europe to the Holy Land and returned to preserve the tradition of round-church building in their native lands. Cambridge's version was put up shortly after 1130 by a small order of 'canons regular' and dedicated to the Holy Sepulchre. Inside, the Round Church retains the form of its original Norman ambulatory, with eight columns and arches in a rather tight circle featuring decorative carving, much of the actual detail dating from restoration during the nineteenth century. The building had been altered and extended to the east in the 1400s, with the addition of gothic windows, a polygonal lantern, and wooden angels which survive in the chancel and north aisle; but was considerably modified and enlarged again in 1841 by Anthony Salvin, who restored to it a turreted roof and rounded windows, and who built a new bell tower which can be seen outside to the north east of the main rotunda.

Map G5 Union Society

Convened during its early years in rooms at the back of an inn, the Cambridge Union Society moved in 1866 to a purpose-built terracotta and red-brick structure characteristic of its architect Alfred Waterhouse, lying at the end of a path beside the Round Church. Founded in 1815, the Society is the University debating club where budding politicians and other public figures have tested their speaking skills. The Union has a President, who sits during debates on a dais and observes the speakers

41

who are given the floor on one or other side. An audience of students and other members votes (like members of the British parliament) by walking through the 'Ayes' or the 'Noes' door to show which side of the debate has persuaded them. Presidents of the Union have included William Whewell, John Maynard Keynes, R. A. Butler, Archbishop Michael Ramsey and Norman St John Stevas. A regular cycle of debates still takes place in the traditional manner each week during term.

38 Central Cambridge from the west across Trinity Backs

(photo courtesy of University of Cambridge Air Photograph Library)

St Edward's Passage to Trumpington Street

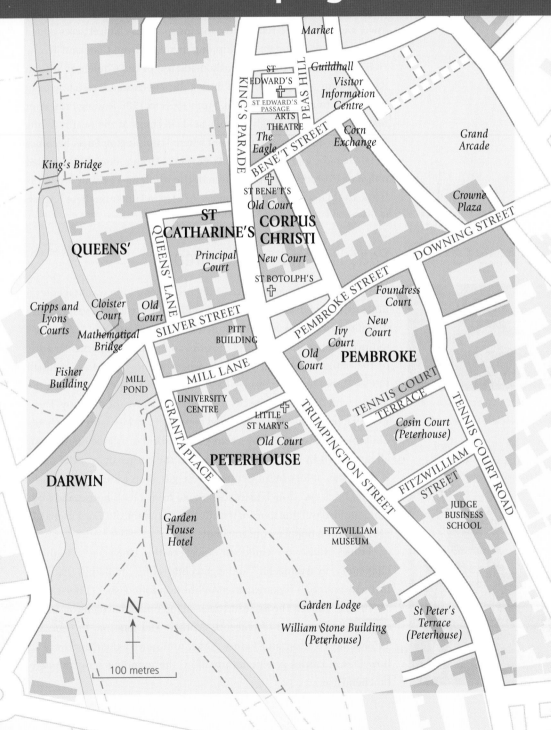

Market

St Edward's

Guildhall

Visitor Information Centre

KING'S PARADE

ST EDWARD'S PASSAGE

ARTS THEATRE

The Eagle

BENE'T STREET

PEAS HILL

Corn Exchange

Grand Arcade

King's Bridge

ST BENE'T'S

Old Court

ST CATHARINE'S

CORPUS CHRISTI

Crowne Plaza

QUEENS' LANE

QUEENS'

Principal Court

New Court

DOWNING STREET

ST BOTOLPH'S

PEMBROKE STREET

Foundress Court

Cripps and Lyons Courts

Cloister Court

Old Court

SILVER STREET

PITT BUILDING

Ivy Court

New Court

Mathematical Bridge

Old Court

PEMBROKE

Fisher Building

MILL POND

MILL LANE

TENNIS COURT TERRACE

TENNIS COURT ROAD

UNIVERSITY CENTRE

LITTLE ST MARY'S

Cosin Court (Peterhouse)

GRANTA PLACE

Old Court

TRUMPINGTON STREET

FITZWILLIAM STREET

DARWIN

PETERHOUSE

JUDGE BUSINESS SCHOOL

Garden House Hotel

FITZWILLIAM MUSEUM

N

Garden Lodge

St Peter's Terrace (Peterhouse)

William Stone Building (Peterhouse)

100 metres

Map F8

St Edward's Church

The Church of St Edward King and Martyr occupies an attractively secluded square surrounded by antiquarian bookshops, accessible via a passage just to the north west of the Visitor Information Centre near Market Square. It dates from 1400, with earlier traces including the lower west tower of c.1200, and contains spacious chancel aisles added in 1446 to accommodate worshipping members from Clare and Trinity Hall. Both colleges had previously made use of the Church of St John Zachary which was demolished during the site-clearance resulting from Henry VI's foundation of King's. From 1523 to 1525 leading Protestant reformers including Hugh Latimer held meetings at the nearby White Horse Inn, which stood at the point where Trumpington Street becomes King's Parade, and preached in St Edward's from a linenfold-panelled pulpit of 1510 surviving in the church. The whole area became known as 'Little Germany', due to the influence of Martin Luther on these English thinkers.

Map F8

Peas Hill and market area

39 Cambridge city arms
(photo by Chris McLeod)

40 Wheeler Street, and the Corn Exchange
(photo by Marc Anderson)

The neighbouring market place is much smaller than it was in medieval times, when St Edward's would have stood on the edge of a vast expanse of stalls stretching as far as the churches of Holy Trinity and St Andrew's to the east. Street-names reflect the original functions of particular areas of the market, including Peas Hill, where we now find the Guildhall (1936-7), home of Cambridge City Council, its façade overlooking the market with the arms of the city of Cambridge above the doorway. These were granted to the city in 1575 and consist of a bridge with three boats underneath, surmounted by a bridge in the form of a castle on the crest, all supported by two sea-horses. Around the corner in Wheeler Street is the Visitor Information Centre, whose gift shop features a sixteenth-century brick and clunch fireplace rescued from a local house, and from where guided walking tours of the city begin; and the old Corn Exchange (1875), now a popular concert venue.

Fisher House on Guildhall Street is the University's Catholic chaplaincy, in seventeenth- and eighteenth-century buildings that were formerly an inn. It is named after Archbishop John Fisher (1469-1535).

In Bene't Street, The Eagle has been an inn under that name or similar since at least the mid-seventeenth century, and here on 28 February 1953 James Watson and Francis Crick announced their discovery of how D.N.A. carries genetic information, the founding act of modern biochemistry.

Map F8

Arts Theatre

Cambridge's Arts Theatre was opened in 1936 by a group of drama enthusiasts including the great economist John Maynard Keynes, who was a fellow of King's College. Margot Fonteyn danced here on the opening night. Among those using the theatre over the years have been the Cambridge Footlights, the revue group which has produced a string of famous entertainers including Jonathan Miller, Peter Cook, John Cleese, Eric Idle, Clive James, Clive Anderson, Stephen Fry, Emma Thompson, Sandi Toksvig, David Baddiel and Sacha Baron Cohen. A major rebuilding of the theatre took place in 1993-6.

Map F9

St Bene't's Church

This Anglo-Saxon church (dedicated to St Bene't or Benedict) stood before a University ever existed in Cambridge, when much of the land between here and the river was a wet marsh. The rough-hewn tower is the oldest building fabric in the county of Cambridgeshire, revealing the relatively basic architectural techniques characteristic of English builders before the Norman conquest of 1066. Blocks of rubble have been piled together with a rough mortar, protected by neater quoins or cornerstones which alternate horizontally and vertically all the way up the sides of the

41 St Bene't's Church, whose tower is the oldest surviving building in Cambridgeshire

(photo by Chris McLeod)

tower to keep frost and damp out of the vulnerable angles where the side walls join. The twin-apertures in the top section are Saxon windows, low and narrow to avoid undermining the strength of the structure.

Inside, the much-restored gothic nave retains at its west end a splendid Saxon tower arch, heavy pillars surmounted by worn carvings of beasts (this work dating from c.1000). A plaque on the north wall of the tower commemorates Fabian Stedman, born in 1633, who developed the art of change-ringing using the bells in this tower.

St Bene't's originally housed priests who ministered to the inhabitants of a modest river-trading town and witnessed, in the early thirteenth century, the first bands of scholars congregating around its precincts. With the growth of the college system the scholars took over, and in 1352 the new Corpus Christi College adopted St Bene't's as its chapel, a status the church retained until 1579.

Map F9

Corpus Christi College

Entered from Trumpington Street, this second smallest of the central colleges is (like the smallest, Peterhouse) historically among the most interesting. It was founded in 1352 by two citizens' guilds, and although one of the guilds was headed by the Duke of Lancaster, Corpus Christi was regarded as having broken the medieval pattern of foundation by

42 Corpus Christi
Old Court

43 Across New Court to Corpus Christi Chapel
(photo by Marc Anderson)

wealthy aristocrats, clerics, or royal officials – and is indeed the only civic foundation of its kind in Cambridge or Oxford. The college's symbol, a pelican plucking her own breast to feed her young, represents Christ's bodily sacrifice: the emblem may be seen on a shield in the vault of the gateway and in prominent places around the college. Despite its close connection with the citizens of Cambridge, Corpus Christi was nonetheless an early victim of 'town-gown' tensions, and in 1381 a mob of townspeople raided its precincts and burned its charters, in protest at rents levied on them by the college to pay for its upkeep.

Passing into the harmonious New Court (1823-7 by William Wilkins), we see a long neo-gothic library range to our right, containing one of the country's most important collections of medieval books and manuscripts. Many were left by Matthew Parker, who was Master of the college from 1544 and especially influential as Archbishop of Canterbury under Elizabeth I. While in favour of Henry VIII's Reformation of the Church, Parker was a man of strong antiquarian tastes who salvaged numerous manuscripts and books from the despoiled monasteries: the Parker Library here includes the Canterbury Gospels and the best text of the Anglo-Saxon Chronicles.

Opposite the main entrance to the nineteenth-century court a chapel is centrally placed; and the architect Wilkins (whose most famous building was the National Gallery in London) chose to be buried here.

Leaving the court by a passageway in the north-east corner we encounter a more ancient scene. The Old Court of Corpus Christi is indeed the oldest surviving residential range in Cambridge or Oxford, and gives an excellent idea of the atmosphere of a small college during the great wave of early collegiate foundations in the mid-1300s. The buildings round this court have been subsequently expanded, with buttresses and dormer windows added, but the basic fabric (of rubble with clunch facing), the tracery round the lower windows, and the essential shape and size, remain as they were not long after 1352. A plaque on the far wall commemorates the residence in this court of Christopher Marlowe and John Fletcher, leading playwrights of the Elizabethan age and contemporaries of Shakespeare. It is remarkable to reflect that these rooms were already 200 years old by the time Marlowe and Fletcher inhabited them.

A much later literary association was struck up at Corpus Christi when writers Christopher Isherwood (*Goodbye to Berlin*, 1939) and Edward Upward (*Journey to the Border*, 1938) became close friends as undergraduates here.

The passageway in the north-west corner of Old Court was the entrance to the college until the nineteenth century; then as now, it

47

led to the Anglo-Saxon Church of St Bene't, which the original Corpus Christi took as its chapel. In the later fifteenth century a brick corridor was erected to connect the college with the church and for many years Corpus Christi was known unofficially as Bene't College.

Map F9

St Catharine's College

The saint whose name is commemorated by the college on Trumpington Street opposite Corpus Christi is clear from the golden Catharine Wheel surmounting its front gates: St Catharine (the patron saint of scholars) was put to death on a wheel. St Catharine's Hall was established here in 1473 with money provided by the Provost of King's, its larger northern neighbour. It changed its name in 1860, as had Clare in 1856, from 'Hall' to 'College', and its spelling distinguishes it from St Catherine's College in Oxford. The college is known colloquially as 'Cats'.

As also at Clare, the medieval site was cleared in the seventeenth century to make way for a grander four-sided court in the classical style by a member of the Grumbold family of masons. Owing to a shortage of money only three sides were completed, leaving the refreshingly open layout which now recedes from the street and gives an impression of depth (in contrast with the gothic fronts of the other colleges hereabouts), broken only by the well-proportioned gateposts, iron gates, and railings dating from 1779. The chapel on the north side of the lawn is modelled on Christopher Wren's work at Pembroke College; and contains the remains, marked by a black slab on the antechapel floor, of Dr John Addenbrooke, a bursar of St Catharine's who died in 1719 leaving money for the foundation of the Cambridge hospital which now bears his name: see pp.61-2 and 105.

Fronting Trumpington Street north of the entrance to St Catharine's is a college building with first-floor railings which used to be the Bull Inn, a hotel popular with American servicemen during the Second World War; and an archway where Thomas Hobson, the University 'carrier', had his stables from 1570 to 1630. Hobson's job was to rent horses to travellers making the journey to London – travellers who always wanted the best and fastest horses, with the result that these animals were always tired. The carrier devised a strict rotation system where each horse arriving from a journey went to the back of the queue, so that travellers seeking a horse took the next one in line. This became known as 'Hobson's choice' – i.e. no choice at all – a phrase which entered the language on this spot. Behind the archway today, on either side of King's Lane, lies a well-concealed warren of modern buildings (including an underground car park) paid for jointly by St Catharine's and King's Colleges, whose

44 St Catharine's Principal Court

45 St Catharine's College from Trumpington Street (photo by Chris McLeod)

sites the narrow lane divides. This is the only instance in 700 years of a single architectural scheme linking two Cambridge colleges.

In more recent times, St Catharine's invested in an impressive new residential site, St Chad's, in west Cambridge, allowing it to increase its student numbers, and further building works are planned. Honorary fellows of the college include theatre director Peter Hall (1950) and actor Ian McKellen (1958).

Map F9

St Botolph's Church

St Botolph is the patron saint of travellers, and churches dedicated to him are often found at the entrances to towns. The word 'Boston' is a contraction of 'Botolph's Town', applied first to the port of Boston in Lincolnshire and adopted later by Boston, Massachusetts. At a junction of medieval Cambridge (near where Silver Street now joins Trumpington Street) stood the city gates admitting the road from London, next to a church which has existed in much its present form since 1400, with nave and aisles dating from before 1350. Items of interest inside St Botolph's Church include the elaborate octagonal font cover of 1637, a remnant of the taste for decoration encouraged in those years by Archbishop William Laud (whose characterful portrait by van Dyck hangs just down the road in the Fitzwilliam Museum).

Map F10

Pitt Building

Diagonally opposite St Botolph's a large gothic-towered structure, known playfully as the 'Freshers' Church' due to its resemblance in

49

46 Pitt Building

(photo by The
Photographic Unit)

the eyes of new undergraduates to a church building, is in fact the Pitt Building, headquarters of the Cambridge University Press. In the Oriel Room jutting towards the street at first-floor level, the Press (whose bookshop we have seen at 1 Trinity Street: pp.26-7) hosts meetings of the University Press Syndicate at which decisions are taken on the 2,000 or so new books and journals published from here each year. The Syndicate has been meeting in this form to govern the business of the Press since 1733, and was established by Richard Bentley, the great classical scholar, Regius Professor of Divinity, and Master of Trinity College, who re-structured and enlarged the Press as a formal part of the University in the early eighteenth century.

The building (1831-3) was named after British Prime Minister William Pitt the Younger, and housed printing and publishing staff until the Press moved first printing (1963) and then publishing (1981) to its spacious modern site near the railway station. The premises are now largely occupied by facilities (including the ground-floor Darwin and Newton Rooms) available to be hired for functions such as conferences and business events. Other parts are occupied by the University's Office of External Affairs and Communications and by design and typesetting staff from the Press's promotional printing operation.

Map E10 Queens' College

Founded in 1448 next to a Carmelite friary, Queens' is best approached from Queens' Lane (off Silver Street). This was the former Milne Street, one of the central routes through medieval Cambridge, and the fine red-brick gatehouse can be imagined fronting an important thoroughfare. The college is named after two queens (Margaret of Anjou, wife of Henry VI; and Elizabeth Woodville, wife of Edward IV), its plural title nowadays distinguishing it from The (singular) Queen's College in Oxford (named after Philippa, wife of Edward III). The Cambridge foundation owes its origins to a priest called Andrew Dokett, vicar of nearby St Botolph's Church, who enlisted the support of these early royal patrons. The worn keystone on the outer side of the gate is thought to represent Dokett holding the college's founding charter.

The gate and court behind it (1440s) represent the first use of brick as a building material on this scale in collegiate Cambridge, and remain one of the best examples of medieval red-brick architecture in Britain. This too is Cambridge's most perfect surviving execution of the college courtyard concept derived in part from the monastic model, with kitchens, hall, parlour, residential quarters, library, chapel (now part of

47 Queens' College dining hall

48 Cloister Court, Queens'

the library), and gate built into a compact square, private and inward-looking. The red-brick court scheme, adopted later at St John's (whose founding father John Fisher had been President of Queens'), is one of the particular glories of Cambridge.

North of Old Court is the newer college chapel, a good example of late-Victorian church building by G. F. Bodley, with a priceless altar triptych by a Flemish artist of the late fifteenth century.

The medieval dining hall in the west range of Old Court has been enlarged and embellished in subsequent years, notably by the stately neo-classical screens (1732-4), the decorated roof (1875), and the fireplace with overmantel featuring tiles designed by Pre-Raphaelite artists and made by William Morris's company. Screens shielding a window in the middle of the passage may be opened to enable a good view. Records survive of eating arrangements in the old hall – and until 1831, with students getting up rather earlier than today, dinner was scheduled for 3 pm.

Moving west from Old Court, we reach the most attractive of Cambridge's small courtyards, Cloister Court. This was an extension of the original premises, incorporating a covered cloister walk, and in the late sixteenth century the striking Tudor lodge with its upper gallery was added to provide more room for a resident Master (known here as a President) and his guests. Its wooden beams, plaster, and jutting bay windows appealingly complement the cloister ranges of medieval brick. The contrast between the cloister and the lodge catches a moment of transition between the relatively simple, communal character of medieval life and the domestic splendours of the Tudor age. The head of a college would have to entertain royalty or aristocracy – indeed Catherine of Aragon is said to have stayed at Queens' back in 1519, Cardinal Wolsey in 1520 – and facilities were required to cater for the increasingly opulent tastes of the upper classes.

The most famous lodger at Queens' was probably Desiderius Erasmus, the humanist scholar, classicist and theologian, who came to Cambridge from his native Rotterdam and, according to oral tradition, chose the college as a base during his four-year stay (1510-14). Erasmus is said to have prepared his edition of the Greek New Testament here. He recorded his impression of Cambridge in letters to a friend, complaining that:

> I cannot go out of doors because of the plague... I am beset with thieves, and the wine is no better than vinegar... I do not like the ale of this place at all...

From Silver Street, where the road crosses the river, the Queens' Mathematical Bridge, built originally in 1749 by James Essex, may be viewed. The present version (1904) is the third on the site to be constructed to an identical design. The building on the corner immediately to our right is also by Essex, and beyond it overlooking Silver Street at the bend in the road is the small tower where Erasmus reputedly lived. The west range of Cloister Court stretches downriver, in medieval brick with gothic window recesses (1460s). To the left a more recent red-brick structure,

49 The Mathematical Bridge

the Fisher Building (1935-6), swings round the corner, bordering to its north a large modern development consisting of Cripps and Lyon Courts. Queens' is the fourth largest college in the University (next to Homerton, Trinity and St John's) in terms of full-time student numbers (including postgraduates), with more than 850.

Map D11 | Darwin College

Founded in 1964 and achieving collegiate status in 1965, Darwin, at the western end of Silver Street, was the first modern Cambridge college designed solely for postgraduates. Cambridge – unlike Oxford (whose All Souls survived from the Middle Ages as a college devoted to higher-level study) – had no such institution remaining. The establishment was funded by three older colleges (Trinity, St John's and Caius), partly in order to relieve their own increasing postgraduate load and partly in response to a recognised shortage of places in Cambridge for postgraduate students. A picturesque site was found at the southern end of the Backs in houses lately vacated by the Darwin family (descendants of famous naturalist Charles Darwin), which gave its name to the new graduate institution – the first Cambridge college to accept both men and women together. The Victorian buildings have been tastefully

53

augmented in a development flanking a leafy byway of the River Cam, just above the Mill Pond.

With the exception of Homerton, Darwin has the highest number of postgraduate students (nearly 600) of any college in the University. Overseas students drawn from over 50 countries make up half of its membership.

<table>
<tr><td>Map E11</td></tr>
</table>

Mill Pond and University Centre

Laundress Lane joins Silver Street to Mill Lane, where the Mill Pond is a popular base for punters, whose escapades can be viewed from adjacent lawns. On Granta Place, the concrete-framed University Centre (1964-7), affectionately known as the 'Grad Pad' (reflecting its origin in the old Graduates' Club), provides eating and entertainment facilities overlooking the river for graduate students, visiting scholars, senior members of the University, and University staff.

<table>
<tr><td>Map F10</td></tr>
</table>

Pembroke College

Opposite the other end of Mill Lane stands the third oldest of the colleges, founded in 1347 by Marie de Valence, widow of the Earl of Pembroke, a wealthy lady descended from the royal families of both England and France. Like other aristocratic women before and after her, she considered the foundation of a college of learning a worthwhile use

50 Pembroke Street
(photo by Marc Anderson)

of her money, endowing it (originally under the name Pembroke Hall) with generous sums. The bicycles of Pembroke students are identified by a letter 'V' for Valence.

Pembroke was the college of the great poet Edmund Spenser, author of *The Faerie Queene*, who came to study here in 1569. Poet Ted Hughes was an undergraduate from 1951 to 1954, as was comedian Peter Cook from 1957 to 1960. Australian writer and entertainer Clive James read English at Pembroke in the 1960s, and has recalled his Cambridge experiences in the memoir *May Week was in June* (1990). The college offers good examples of various architectural styles over 600 years and retains a lived-in feel which some of the neater and prettier colleges lack. Its chapel launched the career of that most famous of English architects, Christopher Wren.

Before crossing the busy junction where Pembroke Street joins Trumpington Street, it is worth pausing to study the various sections of wall along the southern side of Pembroke Street, built shortly after the foundation of the college in 1347. The lighter section, beginning a short distance along the street, reveals the clunchwork as it might have looked in those early years. The brick building nearest the corner is the Old Library, originally the chapel, and the first purpose-built college chapel.

51 West front of Pembroke College Chapel by Christopher Wren

Christopher Wren took up architecture in his thirties having already made a career as a Professor of Astronomy at Oxford. Designed in 1663 and consecrated in 1665, Pembroke Chapel was his first completed

52 Pembroke
College library

building and the first classical-style chapel in Cambridge. Its stone west front overlooks Trumpington Street, framed by Corinthian pilasters and surmounted by a hexagonal lantern; the entrance can be reached via a covered cloister to the right of the porters' lodge inside Old Court. The building was extended eastwards in 1880 by the younger George Gilbert Scott. An ornate plastered ceiling crowns the work, offset to the east by Scott's heavy but not out-of-place marble columns.

A passageway from Old Court leads past the Victorian dining hall into Ivy Court, containing architecture contemporary with Wren (who sent his son to the college in 1691). On the south side of this court there is a coat-of-arms above the window of the first-floor rooms occupied by the poet Thomas Gray from 1756 until his death in 1771; the college possesses an autograph of his 'An Elegy in a Country Churchyard'. The same rooms were occupied by William Pitt the Younger, who became an undergraduate in 1773 before his fifteenth birthday and Prime Minister shortly before his twenty-fifth.

From Ivy Court another arch gives access to the extensive gardens. The path ahead is Ridley's Walk, loved by the Protestant martyr Nicholas Ridley, Master of the college, who in his farewell to it from prison, shortly before his martyrdom in 1555, recalls learning much of St Paul's and other Epistles by heart in the adjacent orchard. The path leads to New Court, by the younger George Gilbert Scott, on the left. Turning right towards the south-east corner of the site, one comes to Foundress Court, a fine modern building (1997) designed by Eric Parry, containing student rooms and the Master's lodge.

From here one may proceed back down the Avenue, with its splendid plane trees, towards the library, with its distinctive clocktower and a statue of Pitt outside. This is one of four buildings designed by Alfred Waterhouse in a period of rapid expansion of the college in the 1870s.

Pembroke is now a medium-sized college with a total of around 650 students.

Map F10 Little St Mary's Church

This church was once known as St Peter's, a name it gave to Peterhouse, the college with which it is linked by a gallery to the south. Although re-consecrated in honour of the Virgin Mary in 1352, the new St Mary the Less retained a connection with Peterhouse, serving as its college chapel until 1632. The east window facing Trumpington Street is a particularly fine example of the flowing tracery of the decorated gothic period, dating from the rebuilding of the church (1340-52). Inside, there is a tablet to former vicar of the parish Godfrey Washington (1670-1729), a great uncle of the first President of the United States whose family arms of stars, stripes, and an eagle, carved here in 1736, were adapted in 1776 for the American flag and crest. Previous priests include the poet Richard Crashaw (here 1638-43).

A delightful churchyard at the back, somewhat overgrown, adjoins the north-facing wall of Peterhouse with its medieval stone and brickwork. Beside the churchyard, Little St Mary's Lane contains, like Botolph Lane and Portugal Place elsewhere in the city centre, rows of attractive house frontages preserving their original line.

Map F11 Peterhouse

In 1984 Peterhouse celebrated its 700th anniversary as the oldest of the colleges. It is also the smallest of those situated in central Cambridge, with just under 400 students.

The establishment of Merton College in Oxford, finalised in 1274, had provided a precedent for a group of scholars sharing premises under

53 Peterhouse Chapel

a set of governing statutes which allowed them a more co-ordinated existence in the service of scholarship. In 1280 the Bishop of Ely set up a foundation in the precincts of St John's Hospital, Cambridge (where St John's College now stands) and in 1284 it moved to its own site next to the Church of St Peter (now called Little St Mary's), whose name it took, along with a royal charter (1285) establishing it with an independent identity similar to that of Merton. The mode of life thus established, centring on the key concepts of lodging, library, and dining room, still dominates Cambridge (now with 31 colleges) more than seven centuries later.

Peterhouse (never known as Peterhouse College, though often in the eighteenth and early-nineteenth centuries referred to as St Peter's College) retains traces of its original thirteenth-century buildings, visible around the southern doorway of the old hall and reached via a passageway between the hall and kitchens on the south side of Old Court. These stone walls, much embellished and extended in later years, are the earliest surviving college building fabric in Cambridge. The hall is better viewed from the north where its later oriel window, ashlar, and lantern dominate Old Court. Despite the alterations, we may imagine a hall on something like this scale, the very first of its kind in Cambridge, accommodating daily groups of dining scholars 700 years ago as it still does today.

Into its small eastern court Peterhouse fits three important buildings: the chapel, extending almost to the street; north of it, the neo-classical Fellows' (or Burrough's) Building; and, flush with the street at the porters' lodge end, the red-brick Perne Library (1593-c.1640). The Fellows' Building (1738-42) is a sedate structure in the Palladian style, housing senior members and designed by James Burrough. The poet Thomas Gray, who had a paranoid fear of fire, lived on the top floor and had a metal bracket fixed outside his window (it can still be seen on the north side), supporting a strap to lower himself to the ground in the event of a conflagration. Provoked by an incident in which a fellow-lodger taunted him by shouting "Fire!", and feeling that he lacked sympathetic friends in Peterhouse, Gray moved across the road to Pembroke College in 1756. Another Peterhouse-Pembroke connection is provided by the friendship and linked careers of physicists Lord Kelvin, who entered Peterhouse in 1841 and later gave his name to the absolute scale of temperature, and George Gabriel Stokes, who was a near-contemporary at Pembroke and after whom important laws in hydrodynamics and fluorescence are named.

Peterhouse Chapel (1628-32) has, at either end, a gothic window, classical pediment, and baroque scrolls, reflecting the taste of the Masters

54 Past Peterhouse porters' lodge towards the Master's lodge

55 Peterhouse dining hall

who sponsored and completed it, Matthew Wren (uncle of Christopher) and John Cosin. At a time when Puritanism, with its plain, simple style, was in the ascendant, Wren and Cosin controversially upheld 'high church' conventions such as the burning of incense, bowing to the altar, and lighting of candles before a crucifix.

More recently, Peterhouse was a pioneer among the colleges in installing electric light. This was arranged for the six-hundredth anniversary celebrations in 1884 by Lord Kelvin. Later fellows of Peterhouse have been Frank Whittle, the inventor of the jet engine, and Max Perutz, John Kendrew, and Aaron Klug, all Nobel Prize winners in molecular biology. Peterhouse has been the home of novelist Kingsley Amis, who taught English here in the early 1960s, and of politician and broadcaster Michael Portillo, who was an undergraduate. Women were admitted as undergraduates in 1985. Although the college's name was adapted for the title of a well-known satirical novel about Cambridge life, *Porterhouse Blue* (1974), the book's author, Tom Sharpe, was actually an undergraduate at Pembroke, and his satire is not based on any particular college.

Across the street from the porters' lodge, behind a wall and an ornate gate, an elegant three-storeyed town house of 1702, with warm, light-red brickwork, was bequeathed to Peterhouse by its builder and is used to accommodate the college's fortunate Master during his term in office. Recent Masters have included eminent historian Hugh Trevor-Roper (Lord Dacre), who lived here from 1980 to 1987 and who formed part of a distinguished tradition of historical studies in the college also represented by Herbert Butterfield, Denis Brogan, David Knowles and Maurice Cowling. In the adjacent building further south, Peterhouse accommodated the London School of Economics and Political Science during its retreat from London in the Second World War.

By the kerb outside Peterhouse, visitors should be careful not to step into 'Hobson's conduit', a channel cut along the side of the road which was designed originally in the early seventeenth century to carry fresh water from the hills to the south, and sponsored by University carrier Thomas Hobson. The elaborate fountain-head, which was in the middle of the market place between 1614 and 1856, now stands as a monument to Hobson where Trumpington Street joins Lensfield Road.

Map G11   Fitzwilliam Museum

56 Portico of the Founder's Building, Fitzwilliam Museum

The Fitzwilliam is the principal museum of the University of Cambridge and contains an internationally important collection of paintings, antiquities, and other works which make it one of eastern England's premier sites for art lovers. Opened in 1848, it is funded both by the

University and by special endowments and trusts, and is a public museum. Over half a million objects and artefacts are kept in five curatorial departments: Antiquities, Applied Arts, Coins & Medals, Manuscripts & Printed Books, and Paintings, Drawings & Prints. Many of its treasures have been bequeathed over the years, and the museum takes its name from its first benefactor, the Seventh Viscount Fitzwilliam of Merrion, whose gift to the University of his works of art and library, together with £100,000 to house them, was received in 1816. Another eminent early patron was the writer and art critic John Ruskin, who in 1861 gave 25 watercolours by J. M. W. Turner. The imposing neo-classical Founder's Building with its gigantic portico and steps rising above the street was designed by George Basevi and built between 1837 and 1875, and later additions include the Marlay Wing which opened in 1924, followed in 1931 by the Courtauld galleries.

Among the treasures which today attract scholars and visitors from around the world are extensive holdings of Greek, Roman, and especially medieval coins; one of the foremost existing collections of prints by Rembrandt; some of the best works by William Blake; paintings including Domenico Veneziano's *Annunciation*, Titian's *Venus Crowned by Cupid, with a Lute Player*, Tintorettos's *The Adoration of the Shepherds*, Veronese's *Hermes, Herse and Aglauros*, and others by Rubens, van Dyck, Tiepolo, Canaletto, Hogarth, Gainsborough, Stubbs, Delacroix, Cézanne, Monet and Renoir; and exhibits of ceramics, sculpture, portrait miniatures, manuscripts, antiquities from ancient Egypt, Greece, Rome and Cyprus, fans and oriental art.

A series of first-class exhibitions may be visited at the Fitzwilliam Museum, supplementing the permanent collection, and there is a well-stocked shop and cafeteria in the glazed courtyard opened in 2004. The museum also offers a wide-ranging programme of events and educational activities for all ages.

Map H11

Judge Business School (Old Addenbrooke's Hospital Site)

Slightly to the south of the Fitzwilliam Museum, on a site lying back from the east side of Trumpington Street and now thoroughly redeveloped by the University, stood the original Addenbrooke's Hospital. Constructed in 1740 with funds left by Dr John Addenbrooke, a physician of St Catharine's College, the hospital survived here until modern times when it was removed to its present position two miles further south, where Hills Road heads out of urban Cambridge (see p.105).

The old site is now home to the Judge Business School, formerly the Judge Institute of Management Studies, founded in 1990 and occupying the spectacularly refurbished main hospital building which The Queen opened in 1996. A department of the University, the School is named after Sir Paul Judge, a leading figure in British financial services whose benefaction led to its foundation, and offers M.B.A.s to business students from all over the world. The front part of the site also now accommodates the Trade Union Centre and Disability Resource Centre.

57 Old Addenbrooke's Hospital in 1870. It was remodelled in 1931, again in the mid-1990s, and is now the Judge Business School

(lower photo by Marc Anderson)

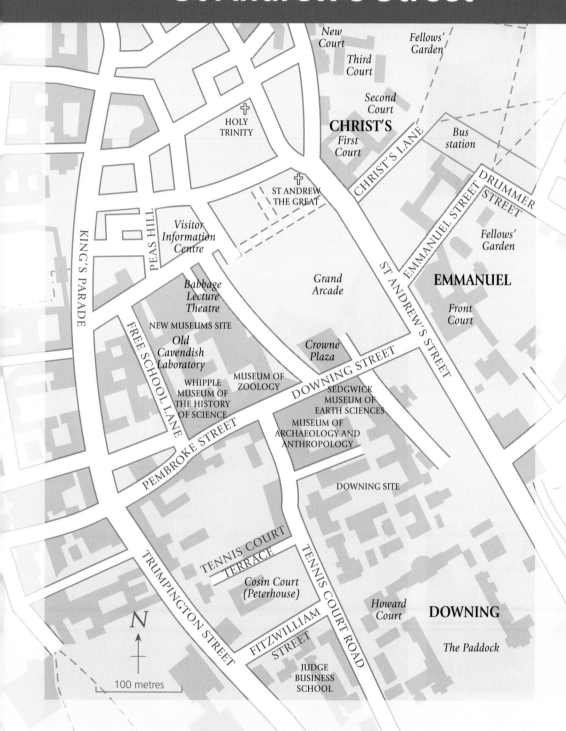

New Court

Third Court

Fellows' Garden

Second Court

HOLY TRINITY

CHRIST'S

First Court

CHRIST'S LANE

Bus station

DRUMMER STREET

EMMANUEL STREET

Fellows' Garden

ST ANDREW THE GREAT

Visitor Information Centre

PEAS HILL

KING'S PARADE

Grand Arcade

ST ANDREW'S STREET

EMMANUEL

Front Court

Babbage Lecture Theatre

NEW MUSEUMS SITE

Old Cavendish Laboratory

FREE SCHOOL LANE

Crowne Plaza

WHIPPLE MUSEUM OF THE HISTORY OF SCIENCE

MUSEUM OF ZOOLOGY

DOWNING STREET

SEDGWICK MUSEUM OF EARTH SCIENCES

MUSEUM OF ARCHAEOLOGY AND ANTHROPOLOGY

PEMBROKE STREET

DOWNING SITE

TRUMPINGTON STREET

TENNIS COURT TERRACE

Cosin Court (Peterhouse)

TENNIS COURT ROAD

Howard Court

DOWNING

N

FITZWILLIAM STREET

JUDGE BUSINESS SCHOOL

The Paddock

100 metres

Free School Lane and New Museums Site

Free School Lane runs south from Bene't Street and offers, from a point just in front of the Old Cavendish Laboratory, a fine perspective on medieval Cambridge. Here we look across the eastern range of Corpus Christi College's Old Court, where the ancient walls of the original lodgings stand back from the street. Behind these windows students have lived continuously for 650 years; and above them, beyond the roof, the tower of St Bene't's (c.1000) reaches back even further into history. Free School Lane is named after the Perse School (now located on Hills Road) which was opened here in 1618 by a bequest of Stephen Perse of Caius College.

58 Looking south into Free School Lane
(photo by Marc Anderson)

59 Across Corpus Christi Old Court to St Bene't's, from Free School Lane

The Old Cavendish Laboratory, founded by and named after William Cavendish, Seventh Duke of Devonshire, is commemorated by a plaque on the wall behind us. In 1874 Cambridge's pioneer laboratory of experimental physics was founded in these Victorian buildings, which for the next 100 years would witness a series of important events in the fields of physics and molecular biology. The labs were established under James Clerk Maxwell who became the University's first Professor of Experimental

60 The Old Cavendish Laboratory at left

Physics in 1871. Here in 1897 J. J. Thomson discovered the electron, and in 1919 his most famous pupil, Ernest Rutherford, returned to the Cavendish to pursue his studies of the composition of the atom, which would prove crucial to the development of nuclear physics. Here in 1932 James Chadwick discovered the neutron, while the 1930s saw the first artificial splitting of the atom at the Cavendish. And here in 1953 Francis Crick and James Watson produced their famous paper suggesting for the first time that the double-helix structure of D.N.A. might provide a mechanism whereby genetic material could be copied from cell to cell and generation to generation, thus giving rise to modern genetic engineering. The work of these laboratories has now removed to larger sites, but the Old Cavendish building remains as a monument to such scientific breakthroughs and to no fewer than 22 Nobel Prize winners between 1904 and 1973.

Near the Cavendish plaque an archway leads during University business hours to the New Museums Site, a cluster of buildings where until the 1840s the Botanic Garden lay. The middle of the nineteenth century saw rapid developments in the study of science, and the University of Cambridge led the way. The term 'scientist' was coined by a Cambridge Professor, William Whewell, in 1833, and Natural Sciences became part of the University curriculum under his guidance, winning approval in 1851. The forward-looking leadership of Albert, the Prince Consort, who was Chancellor of the University from 1847 to 1861, facilitated the pace of change, as did a Royal Commission of 1850 which investigated the function of the ancient universities and resulted in new statutes for Cambridge. New disciplines like geology and zoology began to emerge, inspired by the work of thinkers such as Adam Sedgwick, the pioneer geologist who also battled for liberal reforms (such as the abolition of religious 'tests' limiting degrees to Anglicans) within the University; and his pupil Charles Darwin, who had been an undergraduate in Cambridge. Between 1863 and 1914 the land to the east of Free School Lane was increasingly filled with buildings housing science faculties and laboratories, and this remains the hub of scientific Cambridge.

61 Eric Gill's crocodile on the Mond Building
(photo by Chris McLeod)

Inside the Free School Lane entrance, the Mond Building just to our right (1932, refurbished in 2007) now accommodates the School of the Humanities & Social Sciences and Centre of African Studies. A crocodile cut into the curved brick surface to the right of the doors is the work of English sculptor and engraver Eric Gill, commissioned by his friend, the distinguished Soviet physicist Peter Kapitza in reference to his nickname for pioneering nuclear physicist Ernest Rutherford, since:

> in Russia the crocodile is the symbol for the father of the family and is also regarded with awe and admiration because it has a stiff neck

and cannot turn back. It just goes straight forward with gaping jaws – like science, like Rutherford.

Until recently this site also housed the University Computer Laboratory (now moved to West Cambridge), near the Babbage Lecture Theatre named after Charles Babbage (1792-1871), the pioneer computer scientist who was Lucasian Professor of Mathematics here. A plaque on the wall at the base of the Theatre steps commemorates the first computer calculation executed on the EDSAC (Electronic Delay Storage Automatic Computer) by Maurice Wilkes on 6 May 1949: see also pp.96-7.

Back on the street, at the end of Free School Lane, Botolph House leans rather precariously to the east: evidence of the King's Ditch, a defensive channel which surrounded the medieval town and which was probably dug before 1066. It survives here beneath the building's foundations.

Map G9

Whipple Museum of the History of Science

Nearby on Free School Lane, beneath an arch proclaiming the former Laboratory of Physical Chemistry, lies the entrance to one of the top five museums of its kind in the country. Robert Stuart Whipple (former chairman of the Cambridge Scientific Instrument Company, which had been founded by Charles Darwin's son Horace) gave his private collection of scientific instruments to the University in 1944, inaugurating an archive which is now part of the Department of History and Philosophy of Science. Dating mainly from the sixteenth to twentieth centuries, the display items include early mathematical

62 Whipple Museum entrance, Free School Lane

63 Old Cavendish elementary science class, before 1911

(from *A History of the Cavendish Laboratory 1871-1910*, 1910: photo courtesy of Cambridge University Library)

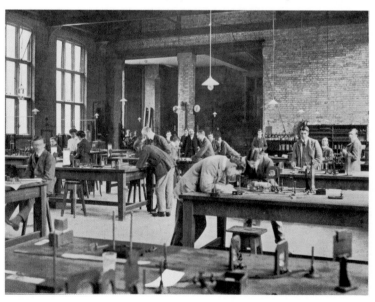

instruments such as astrolabes and sundials, navigation and surveying equipment, electrical measuring instruments, astronomical telescopes, microscopes, spectroscopes and balances. A Victorian parlour and special astronomy section have been laid out on the upper of the museum's two floors.

Map G9

Museum of Zoology

To the east on Pembroke Street, the main entrance to the New Museums Site lies opposite the top of Tennis Court Road. On the site, diagonally across from this gateway, is a museum which has formed part of the University's Department of Zoology since 1938. The staff are active in University teaching and research. The museum holds more than a million specimens, but the displays are spaciously presented: a necessity in the case of the giant spidercrab, elephant seal, leatherback turtle, giant ground sloth and numerous whales which are among exhibits including skeletons of birds such as Darwin's Rhea, and the fish he collected from his voyages on the *Beagle*. It is worth mounting the steps next to the entrance to view at close hand the huge Finback Whale skeleton occupying the podium.

Map H10

Downing Site

64 The Cambridge emblem, with Latin motto exhorting students to drink from the fount of light, wisdom and knowledge

Downing Street is the eastern continuation of Pembroke Street. Between 1896 and 1902 Downing College sold sections of its land to the University, which needed more space to accommodate the fast-growing scientific component of its curriculum. The site now entered from Downing Street or Tennis Court Road was developed between 1903 and 1939 and houses major science departments including those of Anatomy, Earth Sciences, Experimental Psychology, Genetics, Geography, Pathology, Physiology, and Plant Sciences. An architectural highlight is the McDonald Institute for Archaeological Research (1994). The south-eastern perimeter of the site affords the best view of the unusual apsidal end of Downing College chapel.

Map H9

Museum of Archaeology and Anthropology

Of principal interest to visitors are the museums, beginning with the Museum of Archaeology and Anthropology (to the right of the Downing Site entrance). Part of the Faculty of Archaeology and Anthropology, this originated in the 1880s, moving to its present site during the First

World War. Its curatorial staff also teaches and undertakes research in the University. Part of the collection focuses on local antiquities, and finds from the East Anglian area are displayed in quantity. However, items from a range of cultures past and present are contained in this well laid-out building on three floors, including weapons, tools, totem poles, tribal masks, pottery and grave relics. There are Neolithic bows and arrows, Romano-British tombstones, and Maori war canoes.

Map H9

Sedgwick Museum of Earth Sciences

To the left of the Downing Site entrance, at the top of the steps, is a museum named after nineteenth-century scientist Adam Sedgwick (1785-1873), containing one of the world's leading fossil collections, as well as dinosaur skeletons, and the oldest intact collection of geological relics, which belonged to John Woodward (1665-1728). This collector also gave his name to the Woodwardian Professorship of Geology in Cambridge, held in the nineteenth century by Sedgwick, who inaugurated the teaching of geology in the University and counted Charles Darwin among his students. In 1859 Darwin sent his former professor a copy of his *On the Origin of Species*, causing Sedgwick, who cannot have thought that this would become one of the most influential works ever written, to reply:

> I have read your book with more pain than pleasure. Parts of it I admired greatly, parts I laughed at till my sides were almost sore; other parts I read with absolute sorrow, because I think them utterly false and grievously mischievous.

The museum, first opened in 1904, was re-modelled in 2002 and is now a first-class educational resource for visitors of all ages, with a layout that proceeds chronologically through geological time from the Cambrian period to the present day, demonstrating the evolution of the Earth and of life forms through its display of rocks.

65 Adam Sedgwick (1785-1873): portrait by Lowes Dickenson, 1867

(courtesy of the Sedgwick Museum of Earth Sciences)

Map I10

Downing College

Built on a 15-acre site, Downing is the most spacious of the central colleges, its vast lawns stretching away from the neo-classical forecourt. The grounds afford an unexpected impression of grandeur when entered via the claustrophobic bustle of Regent Street (the southern continuation of St Andrew's Street). This college was founded in 1800, with money provided for the purpose in the will of Sir George Downing, grandson of the man who built Downing Street, the London residence of the British Prime Minister. Downing died in 1749, legal wrangles over his will

66 Downing College

preventing its proper execution for 50 years. The foundation came after a very long lull, no new college having been established in Cambridge since Sidney Sussex in 1596.

The imposing buildings on three sides of the lawns are in the Greek classical style, and were begun by William Wilkins, who had travelled in Greece and was instrumental in the neo-classical revival of the early nineteenth century: his work at Downing was executed between 1807 and 1820. The north side of the quadrangle was finally closed off in 1953 with the building of the chapel. Work has continued on the site, still faithful to Wilkins's style, and three major newer buildings by Quinlan Terry are to be found near the west and east gates, striking attempts to preserve a classical idiom in modern Cambridge architecture. On the Tennis Court Road side, the Howard Building (1987) is used as a centre for receptions, conferences, and entertainments, and the adjacent Howard Court (1994) is a residential building; while near the Regent Street gate the Library Building (1993) adopts a colonnaded portico fronting a symmetrical plan capped by an octagon recalling the Tower of the Winds in Athens. Symbols carved on the building's frieze

69

were selected by Downing's fellows to represent subjects studied in the library, including Modern Languages (a tower of Babel), English (a laurel wreath), History (an hour glass), Astronomy (a radio telescope), and Biology (a D.N.A. double helix). The whole, like much else in Downing and in Cambridge at large, is built in rich Ketton stone.

The north-western corner of the courts, along from the Howard Building, affords an inspiring view across Downing's Paddock. The prominent spire that sets off the southern end of the lawns belongs to the Roman Catholic Church of Our Lady and the English Martyrs (1885-90) on Hills Road.

Downing was the college of the influential literary critic F. R. Leavis (1895-1978).

Map 19   Emmanuel College

On St Andrew's Street opposite the end of Downing Street we find Emmanuel College, whose Front Court, beyond the porters' lodge, presents one of the best perspectives in Cambridge. These wide arcades provide a vantage from which the façade of Christopher Wren's chapel (1666-79) appears in fine proportion on the other side of the lawn. A pediment with clock, lantern, and cupola rises above Corinthian

67 Emmanuel College gardens

68 Christopher Wren's Emmanuel College Chapel

columns and pilasters interspersed with swags and garlands. The baroque effect of the ornamental carving is kept in check by a neat row of windows at first-floor level, behind which a gallery runs across the entire width of the court, supported on the open arcade below. Square and circular motifs play off each other and the result is a well-balanced composition further enhanced in certain lights by the pale rosy glow on the Ketton stone brought by Wren from Northamptonshire. This was Wren's second project in Cambridge (after Pembroke Chapel) and he designed it in the same year (1666) that he witnessed the Great Fire of London and decided to pursue a full-time career as an architect, having previously distinguished himself as a scientist and Oxford professor.

Emmanuel College had been founded in 1584 on the site of a Dominican friary dissolved at Henry VIII's Reformation of the English Church, and from the start it was a severely Protestant establishment with an inclination towards Puritanism. A training-ground for young pastors and preachers of a Calvinist persuasion, it came under pressure during the conservative backlash led by Archbishop Laud in the 1630s, and many Emmanuel men sailed away to plant new colonies on the east coast of America where they could pursue their religion in their own way. More than 30 of the first 100 university graduates to settle in New England in the generation after the Pilgrim Fathers were from Emmanuel – among them John Harvard, who helped to endow a new educational establishment in Newtown, Massachusetts, which came to bear his name (he is commemorated by a plaque in the passage leading into the antechapel and by a stained glass window). The settlement's first pastor was Thomas Shepard, in whose honour (as another distinguished product of Emmanuel College) Newtown was re-named Cambridge. The figures in the chapel windows (1884) are designed to illuminate the continuity of church history and the part played in it by members of the college.

Passing from Front Court on the south side of the chapel the visitor reaches the extensive college gardens, landscaped to include a miniature duckpond. This is in fact the fishpond of the old friary, whose thirteenth-century boundary wall, now brick-clad, can be identified to the south, beyond the croquet and tennis lawns. There too is a large building of 1910, now the college library; and to the viewer's right a red-brick range erected in the 1630s to meet a rapid growth in student numbers. North of the duckpond a gate leads into the Fellows' Garden which contains some very fine trees: to the right, a 200-year-old oriental plane; directly ahead, a massive copper beech; and in front of it an oak planted by The Queen to mark the college's four-hundredth anniversary. The garden also contains an outdoor swimming pool, concealed behind the trees on a site used for bathing since at least 1690. A modern sculpture, *The Jester*, is by Wendy Taylor.

Aside from the chapel, Emmanuel's best architecture belongs to the eighteenth century, including the Westmorland Building on the south side of Front Court (named after the sixth Earl of Westmorland, a direct descendant of the college's founder Walter Mildmay), and the elegantly panelled dining hall (an adaptation by James Essex of what had been the original Dominicans' church), which may be seen via a door in the north-west corner. A passage leads beyond the hall into a further court containing at its far end the Old Library, which served as the college's first chapel and until 1930 as its library, and which retains its original oak screen. In 1996 The Queen's Building, housing a theatre, was built of Ketton stone overlooking the Fellows' Garden.

| Map H7 | # Christ's College |

The carved heraldry above Christ's College gateway on St Andrew's Street is almost identical to that of St John's, reminding us that the two colleges were founded at about the same time (Christ's in 1505, St John's in 1511) with benefactions from Lady Margaret Beaufort, whose arms are represented here. The great royal lady (mother of Henry VII) died in 1509 between the two foundation dates, and Christ's has the distinction of having been launched by her in person: she even lived in the Master's lodge for a short time. Astute visitors will notice that the

69 Christ's College: First Court with dining hall

70 New Court with the 'typewriter building'

statue in a niche above the arch is of Lady Margaret herself, whereas the one at St John's is of St John. The broad oak doors beneath Christ's gateway, with their robust linenfold panelling, date from the later Tudor period towards the end of the sixteenth century. In contrast with the East Anglian and south-of-England orientation of many of the earlier colleges, it was ordained that Christ's should take a good proportion of its fellows and students from the north.

Inside we encounter First Court, decorated with flowers for all

71 Beaufort arms beneath the oriel window of the Master's lodge in First Court, Christ's

seasons and colourful even in winter. The court was built quickly (1505-11) in the flush of enthusiasm following Lady Margaret's foundation: in fact her money was being used to renovate and replace an ailing older college on the same site, God's House, established here in 1446. The architectural uniformity of the court belies its actual building history: the original Tudor clunch and brick walls are hidden behind eighteenth-century stone facing and windows, while the prominent Tudor-gothic dining hall on the far side is largely a nineteenth-century replica – although the architect, George Gilbert Scott the younger, was careful to re-use old materials where he could. The wisteria-covered Master's lodge to the left of the hall retains a Tudor oriel window, with original carving, again of the Beaufort arms, beneath it.

Christ's chapel, entered to the left of the lodge, contains high-quality medieval stained glass in its north windows; a portrait of Lady Margaret on the west wall; an unusual window linking the chapel to the Master's lodge, used originally by the foundress to watch mass from her oratory; and a brass eagle lectern of the late fifteenth century, said to be the best of its date in the country.

Through a passage between the hall and the kitchens stands, on the far side of Second Court, the Fellows' Building of 1640-3, an important landmark in Cambridge architecture which inaugurated the taste for classical motifs that would culminate in the Senate-House 80 years later. The identity of the Christ's architect is unknown, but he combined triangular and rounded pediments (see for example the main doors, or the dormer windows jutting from the roof) in an alternating scheme, and framed the building at each corner with an ionic pilaster in a spirit reminiscent of the work of Inigo Jones in London but quite new to Cambridge. This Fellows' Building, along with the main court at Clare, is the most imposing seventeenth-century collegiate structure dating from the years before Christopher Wren came to do his work at Pembroke, Emmanuel and Trinity.

Through the central archway may be seen the beautiful Fellows' Garden, in which poet John Milton, author of *Paradise Lost*, gained inspiration. Milton (known as the Lady of Christ's because of his youthful appearance) was an undergraduate here from 1625 to 1629 and took his M.A. in 1632. Another famous Christ's student was the author of *On the Origin of Species*, Charles Darwin. He came here in 1827, was accommodated in lodgings now marked by a plaque outside Boots on Sidney Street, and later wrote that "No pursuit at Cambridge was followed with nearly so much eagerness or gave me so much pleasure as collecting beetles". South African statesman General Jan Smuts studied at Christ's in the early years of the twentieth century, later becoming Chancellor of the University. Writer and physicist C. P. Snow, whose novel *The Masters* (1951) describes the intrigues of Cambridge college life, was a fellow here until his death in 1980.

Rounding the corner to the north we enter Third Court, with its nineteenth-century range adapting the design of the Fellows' Building. Beyond, the stepped layers of New Court (1966-70) give rise to its affectionate nickname 'the typewriter building'. Christ's is a popular medium-sized college with around 400 undergraduates and 100 postgraduates.

72 The Milton portrait in Christ's dining hall

(courtesy of Master and Fellows of Christ's College)

Map G8

St Andrew the Great Church

This very centrally located church, almost opposite the gatehouse of Christ's College, is a Victorian replacement on the site of a much older church destroyed by fire in 1842. Re-modelled in the mid 1990s, it is now used by the parish of Holy Sepulchre (the Round Church). The building contains a memorial tablet to the family of Captain James Cook, explorer of the South Seas.

Map G7

Holy Trinity Church

Another centrally placed church, at the junction of Market and Sidney Streets, is basically medieval, with parts dating back to the twelfth century and numerous subsequent extensions and embellishments.

73 Holy Trinity Church in the early nineteenth century

(from Ackermann's *A History of the University of Cambridge*, 1815: photo courtesy of Cambridge University Library)

Holy Trinity's slender spire, rebuilt in place of an earlier one in 1901, has long dominated this corner of town. From 1782 to 1836 this was the base of hymn-writer and preacher Charles Simeon (in 1799 one of the founders of the Church Missionary Society), who stamped upon it an Evangelical character which it retains. He is commemorated in the chancel.

Sidney Street and Jesus Lane to Castle Hill

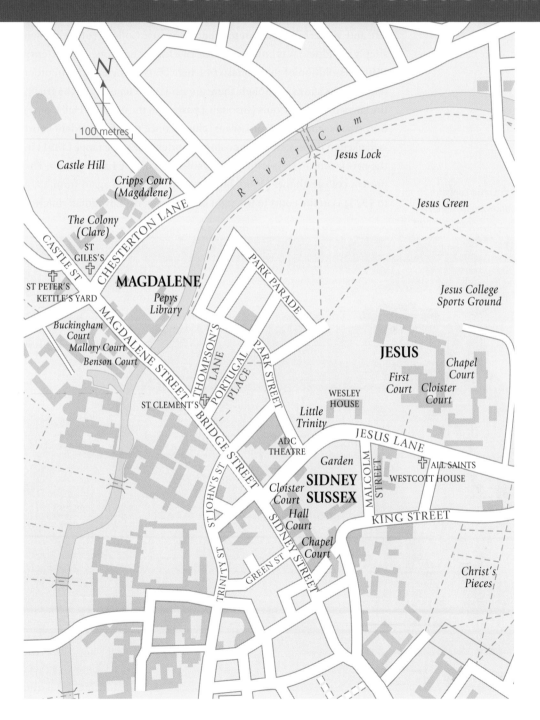

N

100 metres

River Cam

Jesus Lock

Castle Hill

Cripps Court
(Magdalene)

Jesus Green

CHESTERTON LANE

The Colony
(Clare)

ST
GILES'S

CASTLE ST

MAGDALENE

PARK PARADE

Jesus College
Sports Ground

ST PETER'S
KETTLE'S YARD

Pepys
Library

MAGDALENE STREET

THOMPSON'S LANE

PORTUGAL PLACE

PARK STREET

JESUS

Chapel
Court

Buckingham
Court
Mallory Court
Benson Court

First
Court

Cloister
Court

ST CLEMENT'S

BRIDGE STREET

WESLEY
HOUSE

Little
Trinity

ADC
THEATRE

JESUS LANE

ST JOHN'S ST

Garden

MALCOLM STREET

ALL SAINTS
WESTCOTT HOUSE

Cloister
Court

SIDNEY
SUSSEX

Hall
Court

KING STREET

TRINITY ST

GREEN ST

SIDNEY STREET

Chapel
Court

Christ's
Pieces

Sidney Sussex College

Looming behind its wall fronting Sidney Street towards the junction with Jesus Lane, this college is known for its attractive gardens and for the head of Oliver Cromwell which is buried here. A nineteenth-century gothic archway leads past the porters' lodge and opens into two courts, left and right. Like Emmanuel, Sidney Sussex College (often known simply as Sidney) was built on the site of a friary abandoned after Henry VIII's Dissolution of the Monasteries: here friars of the Franciscan order had their lodgings. Although there are no visible remains of the friary, the lawned Cloister Court (through a passage to the north of Hall Court) now stands where the Franciscans' church once was. This verdant court is flanked to the east by an imposing red-brick and stone range (1891) in the neo-Jacobean style with Dutch gables and ornate bay windows. The present college chapel (1600, but rebuilt in 1782 and again from 1912 to 1923) is in the court to the right of the lodge. Its 'Edwardian' interior

74 David Loggan's engraving of Sidney Sussex College in 1690

features attractive brown oak stalls and panels, coloured marble floor, bronze and marble altar, and decorative barrel-vaulting.

Sidney was founded in 1596 by an endowment left in the will of Lady Frances Sidney, Countess of Sussex (aunt of the Elizabethan poet Philip Sidney) in 1588. Its early buildings facing the street were converted in the 1820s and '30s by Sir Jeffrey Wyatville, whose controversial gables and stone facing altered the character of the site and still dominate from most directions. The young Oliver Cromwell had entered Sidney in 1616 and studied here for a year as a fellow commoner of the college, returning to Cambridge in 1643 to establish a garrison of Parliamentarian soldiers during the English Civil War and imprisoning the Master of his old college on account of the man's Royalist sympathies! Sidney accepted in 1960 a wooden cabinet containing an embalmed head impaled on a spiked metal pole – the head of Cromwell himself, preserved after his posthumous decapitation in 1661 and finally buried here 300 years later (commemorated by a plaque in the antechapel).

In the early nineteenth century Sidney gained a reputation for mathematics and science, and built its own chemistry and physics laboratory before the University itself had such facilities. Its gardens, marking the extent of the Franciscans' precinct, stretch to the north and east beyond the main courts and are visible from a covered passageway leading off next to the chapel. Since Loggan's print of 1690, showing the line of the King's Ditch marked by a row of sycamores, buildings have encroached on the site – the latest of them the Mong Building, opened in 1999 – but it remains beautifully kept.

Leaving via the porters' lodge, walking south down Sidney Street and turning left into Sussex Street, we see ahead the college's own modern Bridge of Sighs – a simple but attractive structure of 1991 linking at the upper level two buildings belonging to the college.

Map H5

Jesus College

A few minutes' walk to the north east, off the beaten track for many tourists, the ancient courts of Jesus College are well worth a visit. The first college to take over the site of an old medieval priory, the nunnery of St Radegund, Jesus extended collegiate Cambridge into the fields on the edge of the old city, where it retains, with grounds leading towards the outreaches of the River Cam, a rural air. Dedicated in 1496 to 'the Blessed Virgin Mary, St John the Evangelist, and the Glorious Virgin St Radegund', but soon adopting its other name, associated with Jesus Lane and Jesus parish in which it was situated, Jesus College was the first of many Tudor foundations in Cambridge and Oxford; and one of its early students was a 14-year-old orphan called Thomas Cranmer, later to be the great Tudor divine and author of the Book of Common Prayer.

Entered from Jesus Lane via a walled path known as The Chimney (from the French word 'chemin') and an arch under the castellated red-brick gate-tower of about 1500 featuring a statue of the founder Bishop Alcock beneath his symbol (a cock perched on a globe), the college is built around the plan of the original nunnery buildings. Its highlights are the small Cloister Court, with an atmosphere closer than any other space in Cambridge to that of a medieval religious foundation (though this effect is mediated through several restorations); and the chapel, a smaller version of the original nuns' church, superbly restored and embellished by Victorian craftsmen. The original twelfth- and thirteenth-century fabric of the chapel is the oldest building to be incorporated within a Cambridge college.

75 Jesus College
First Court

76 Jesus College Chapel Court

First Court, reached immediately after the gate-tower and porters' lodge, is a good example of the hybrid but harmonious quality of many college sites in Cambridge. Based on monastic foundations but rebuilt and enlarged in subsequent centuries, its architects over the years have remained sensitive to the aesthetic potential of the site, keeping the west side open (with the exception of a low wall) and preserving a unity among the buildings. The bronze horse on the lawn is by modern sculptor Barry Flanagan; and there are pieces by Eduardo Paolozzi and other well-known sculptors in adjacent parts of the college.

Access to Cloister Court is through a passage to the east. On the far side of this intimate cloister lie the remains, slightly sunken, of the arched doorway into the nuns' Chapter House, with a window on either side sporting stiff-leaf carving of about 1230. A passage just to the right leads to the massive, open-ended Chapel Court.

The darkness of the chapel interior, entered from Cloister Court, is relieved by coloured light filtered through windows in the nave and transepts (1873-7) by the Pre-Raphaelite artists William Morris, Edward Burne-Jones and Ford Madox Brown, and in the chancel (1849-58) by Augustus Pugin. Galleries of Norman arches in the north transept (1150-75) provide indications of the original structure, while the chancel's narrow pointed lancet windows in the early-English gothic style belong to a thirteenth-century scheme much revised by Pugin (famous for his work on the Houses of Parliament), who also rebuilt the choir stalls. The attractive roof-painting in the crossing and nave is by William Morris.

77 'Hope, Faith, Charity': glass in the Jesus College Chapel (photo by Ian Hart)

It is worth ascending from the north-west corner of the cloister to the college hall, originally the refectory of the nunnery, with its roof of Spanish chestnut (c.1500, restored in the nineteenth century).

The Quincentenary Library, opened in 1996 to mark the college's 500th anniversary, and the adjacent accommodation buildings completed in 2000, have created a new court in the south-eastern part of the college. Jesus also owns a very fine Georgian town house known as Little Trinity (c.1725), set back at the end of a small walled garden where Jesus Lane meets Park Street and accommodating postgraduate students. The college houses nearly 750 full-time students (including postgraduates), making it the fifth largest in the University. It admits about 150 undergraduates each year.

Apart from Cranmer, other famous Jesus students have included the writers Laurence Sterne, Samuel Taylor Coleridge, Alistair Cooke, Jacob Bronowski and David Hare; and Prince Edward, who read history here from 1983 to 1986. Sir Arthur Marshall, well-known locally for his pioneering work in the aeronautic industry and his associations with Cambridge Airport, was a Jesus undergraduate in the early 1920s: he died in 2007, aged 103.

Map H5

All Saints Church

78 All Saints,
Jesus Lane
(photo by Chris McLeod)

The impressively spired church opposite Jesus is All Saints, built by G. F. Bodley in 1864. Like Jesus College chapel, it contains stained glass (1865-6) by pre-Raphaelites Morris, Burne-Jones and Madox Brown. Constructed to replace the old All Saints on St John's Street (which stood alongside what is still All Saints Passage), the building remains consecrated but is maintained by the Churches Conservation Trust. With an interior that features wonderful examples of Victorian Arts & Crafts decoration, All Saints has been noted as an important landmark in the use of gothic forms by nineteenth-century English architects and is one of the lesser-known gems of central Cambridge.

Map H5

Westcott House

Next to All Saints lies Westcott House, one of the four independent theological colleges in Cambridge. Here Anglican priests are trained. The college was founded in 1881; its street-facing range, part of a grassy inner court, dates from 1899.

Map G5

Wesley House

Further west, on the opposite side of Jesus Lane, the Methodist theological college Wesley House was established on its present site in 1925, having been founded in 1921. It also now provides a base for inter-faith groups. The newer buildings facing the road date from 1972.

Map G5

A.D.C. Theatre

Across the street from the Jesus College house Little Trinity is the theatre of the University's Amateur Dramatic Club, founded in 1855 and keenly supported by the Prince of Wales (later Edward VII), who arrived at Cambridge as an undergraduate in 1861. The present theatre building was opened in 1935. It stands next to the Quakers' Friends Meeting House.

Map F5

St Clement's Church

Back on Bridge Street, on the way to Magdalene College, we pass the Church of St Clement, who became the patron saint of Danish sailors. This is the part of Cambridge developed by Danish invaders (yet to be Christianised) from c.875 AD: their port lay where Magdalene Bridge crosses the Cam. The present church building dates from after 1218, with many later additions including the street-facing tower of 1821. It now doubles as a Greek Orthodox church dedicated to St Athanasios.

A short detour at this point will take us on one side to the picturesque house-fronts of Portugal Place, and on the other to the Cambridge Jewish Synagogue in Thompson's Lane.

Map E4

Magdalene College

Magdalene was a re-foundation, in 1542, of an older institution in the same buildings: a monastic hostel devoted to the education of scholar-monks. No other Cambridge college has this origin. Buckingham College, as it was known from about 1472, had been endowed on this site by four Benedictine abbeys (whose arms appear over some of the old doorways) and by the family of the dukes of Buckingham, but was dissolved by Henry VIII and re-opened as a secular college of the University with a dedication to St Mary Magdalene (pronounced 'maudlyn', and no doubt striking a chord with the name of its benefactor, Lord Audley, in keeping with the Renaissance love of punning). Original medieval brickwork (1470s) is visible in the range overlooking the river at Magdalene Bridge.

Until the early nineteenth century Magdalene remained the only part of the University on the far side of the river. Always a small college, its annual intake sometimes dwindling into single figures, it did not

79 Magdalene College from the Cam

begin to expand until the early twentieth century under the Mastership of the man who wrote the words of *Land of Hope and Glory*, A. C. Benson. In the modern period Magdalene has attracted many notable figures, including Rudyard Kipling, Thomas Hardy and T. S. Eliot (who were honorary fellows); and I. A. Richards, C. S. Lewis and Michael Ramsey (Archbishop of Canterbury, 1961-74).

Magdalene's entrance lies tight against the street, diagonally opposite the sixteenth-century Pickerel Inn; and in past times this popular corner of town, just inside the entrance to the city at the foot of Castle Hill where the main routes from the north, east and south converge, contained five inns in a row between the porters' lodge and the junction. Through the gate, First Court features a small chapel with a medieval oak roof, and to the left of it on the first floor rooms occupied from 1955 to 1963 by the celebrated Christian apologist C. S. Lewis, who was Professor of Medieval and Renaissance English in the University. On the first floor on 'C' staircase lived the Victorian poet and novelist Charles Kingsley (author of *The Water-Babies*, 1863). To the east of the court stands the hall, where members of Magdalene preserve the ancient tradition of dining each night by candlelight, there being no electricity in the hall. Along with the Old Courts at Corpus Christi and Queens', Magdalene's First Court is the best encapsulation in Cambridge of the original medieval setting of domestic life in a college.

80 The Pepys Library

The architectural highlight of Magdalene, the late seventeenth-

century Pepys Library Building with its attractive colonnaded stone façade in light Ketton stone, is found on the far side of Second Court. The diarist and secretary of the Admiralty Samuel Pepys died in 1703 and left to his college 3,000 volumes (including medieval manuscripts, early printed books by Caxton, Sir Francis Drake's nautical almanack, and his own famous diary), all arranged in the library in order of height. At the south end of the Pepys Building are rooms occupied in the mid-nineteenth century by the Irish nationalist politician C. S. Parnell, on the ground floor because of his tendency to sleep-walk.

Although still among the smaller colleges, with 350 or so undergraduates, Magdalene expanded considerably in the twentieth century, and a site on the other side of the street features Benson, Buckingham, and Mallory Courts – the last named after George Mallory, the Magdalene mountaineer who died in his attempt on Everest of 1924. The long west range of Benson Court was designed in brick by Edwin Lutyens, best known as the planner of New Delhi in India. Closer to the street, early half-timbered buildings have been sensitively incorporated; and around the corner in Chesterton Lane a further extension, Cripps Court, was opened in 2004.

| Map E3 | ## St Giles's Church |

At the south-east corner of Castle Street the large Anglican Church of St Giles dates mainly from 1875, but incorporates old aisle arches bearing witness to the former building on its site which existed from c.1092.

| Map D4 | ## Kettle's Yard |

Kettle's Yard, a combination of a house and gallery not far above the traffic lights on the other side of Castle Street, contains a first-rate collection of twentieth-century art, including works by Henri Gaudier-Brzeska, Ben Nicholson, Barbara Hepworth and Henry Moore. The site was developed in 1957 by art lover Jim Ede from four old cottages, accommodating a collection which he gave to the University of Cambridge (still partly responsible for its maintenance) in 1966. The buildings, extended in the 1970s and again in the mid-1990s, provide an environment which has itself been described as a work of art.

| Map D3 | ## St Peter's Church |

A little further up the hill, tucked away on a grassy bank behind trees, the very small Church of St Peter displays signs of its medieval origins, including a blocked doorway to the north and (inside) a carved font, both remnants of the Norman period. This is a peaceful spot, hidden from the bustling city just beneath it. More energetic visitors might continue up Castle Street to the site of Cambridge Castle itself, beyond the car park of the County Council buildings. All that remains of the castle is a rough motte (1068) commanding a view of the towers and spires it pre-dates.

81 St Peter's Church

5   Outlying sites

82,83 and 84   Schlumberger Building, High Cross Site (top); William Gates Building, West Cambridge Site (left); History Faculty Building, Sidgwick Site (right)

The short entries in this final section relate to sites which lie away from central Cambridge, including all of the remaining University colleges and selected other places of interest connected with the University. They are presented in a roughly clockwise order starting with Newnham College to the south west of the city centre. All are marked on the general map of Cambridge at the beginning of this book. The first seven entries in particular (from Newnham to the University Library) comprise a walkable itinerary for the visitor with a bit more time but without motor transport.

Map B11

Newnham College

One of the most important and influential Cambridge or Oxford college foundations since the sixteenth century, Newnham (1871) set in motion a slow but distinct wave of feminist reform and was soon also setting new academic standards within the University. It has produced many leading women writers, scientists and intellectuals and remains stalwartly an all-women college, with more female undergraduates (c.420) than any other college. Old Newnhamites include Sylvia Plath, Margaret Drabble, A. S Byatt, Rosalind Franklin (who worked with Crick and Watson on the discovery of D.N.A.), Germaine Greer, Lisa Jardine and Oscar-winning actress Emma Thompson.

Newnham's early mentors were Henry Sidgwick, the moral philosopher and Cambridge professor who promoted women's education, and Anne Jemima Clough, its first Principal. The liberal aristocracy took an interest in the foundation, and the earliest students included Prime Minister's daughter Helen Gladstone, and Eleanor Balfour, sister of the future Prime Minister and later Mrs Sidgwick. In 1875 – by which time another women's college, Girton, had already been located in Cambridge – Clough took her growing assembly of students to the present site to the west of the male University. Here a parade of buildings in the Queen Anne style was being constructed by Basil Champneys, with Dutch red-brick gables and white woodwork, well suited to its setting around extensive lawns and flower beds. This is a highly attractive example of the Victorian taste for adapting older architectural styles on a grander scale in new environments, and a women's college presented Champneys with a challenge which he met with success. The scheme did not include a chapel (and the college still does without one).

By 1914 Newnham had more than 200 students, and during the First World War (with men called to serve abroad) it was larger than any of the male colleges. A significant step towards the acknowledgement

85 Newnham College

that a University without women was a University cut off from a high proportion of the nation's intellect came in 1917 when Newnham received a college charter; and another was made in 1948 when women finally received University degrees.

The college library was extended (2004) in keeping with the warm red brick of the nineteenth-century buildings.

Map C11 Ridley Hall

Just east of Newnham stands Ridley Hall, conceived in 1877 as the first (with Wycliffe Hall, Oxford) of the Cambridge and Oxford theological colleges; it opened in 1881. Housed in buildings contemporary with those of Newnham next door, this Anglican college has tended towards the more evangelical end of the theological spectrum.

Map B10 Sidgwick Site

On Sidgwick Avenue opposite Newnham College lies the principal site of the University's non-scientific faculties, named after moral philosopher Henry Sidgwick. Developed initially in the 1960s, it provides lecture

86 Law Faculty Building

rooms and libraries for students of Classics, Economics, English, History, Law, Modern & Medieval Languages, and Philosophy, among others. Close to the road, the Museum of Classical Archaeology contains plaster casts of famous Greek and Roman sculptures including the Parthenon Frieze and the Delphi Charioteer. The collection originated as lecture-aids in the mid-nineteenth century and was first gathered in a museum in 1884, in a building leased from Peterhouse on Little St Mary's Lane, moving to the present site in 1992. The importance of maintaining these replicas was emphasised when a terrorist bomb damaged one of the originals in Florence's Uffizi Gallery in 1993.

On the far side of the site, the History Faculty Building (1964-8) by James Stirling has been one of Cambridge's most controversial, its bricks and bold glass front representing a kind of modern experimentation despised by architectural historian Nikolaus Pevsner, but admired by other critics as a masterpiece of innovation.

Next to it are more recent examples of cutting-edge design, all features of a major expansion of the Sidgwick Site since 1996. In that year The Queen opened the Law Faculty Building (including the Squire Law Library), designed by Sir Norman Foster. In 2000 the Faculty of Divinity moved from St John's Street to new custom-built premises on the western side. The Institute of Criminology arrived in 2004, the same year in which the Faculty of English occupied its new building to the north.

The West Road Concert Hall within the Faculty of Music, designed in the mid-1970s by Sir Leslie Martin (who designed London's Royal Festival Hall), remains a lively venue for classical concerts.

Map A11

Selwyn College

87 Selwyn gatehouse

George Augustus Selwyn, first Anglican Bishop of New Zealand and later Bishop of Lichfield, died in 1878 and was commemorated by the foundation of a new college closely associated with the Church of England. Opening in 1882 on Grange Road, Selwyn College (like its earlier counterpart in Oxford, Keble College) insisted that its senior members be confirmed Anglicans and maintain Christian principles. The Bishop had been a model of Victorian 'muscular Christianity', who as a St John's undergraduate in 1829 had rowed in the first Cambridge crew to race against Oxford and whose "pure and heroic" English virtues were praised by Charles Kingsley in his dedication to *Westward Ho!*. The Greek inscription above the college gateway means 'Stand fast in the faith and acquit yourselves like men'.

Selwyn became a favourite college for the sons of clergymen, different from the other late-Victorian Cambridge establishments (Girton,

88 Selwyn Chapel

Newnham, Fitzwilliam, Homerton, Hughes Hall) which were inspired more by secular and social than ecclesiastical ideals. Its subsequent history has been one of gradual integration into the University. By 1926 it had achieved many of the privileges of the older colleges and in 1958 it was admitted as a full college of the University.

Selwyn's architecture is in the red-brick, neo-Tudor style of the 1880s, with a sturdy, turreted gate-tower in the front range set back from Grange Road and a chapel reminiscent in shape (though not in scale) of the one built at King's College 400 years earlier. To the north of Old Court towards West Road a major building campaign, known as Ann's Court, was inaugurated in 2003.

Map A9

(west of)

Clare Hall

Clare Hall is a graduate college founded by the Master and Fellows of Clare College in 1966. Their decision had been inspired by a proposal two years earlier from Richard Eden, then a fellow of Clare, who became a founding fellow of Clare Hall. He proposed that the college establish a centre for advanced study to bring together an international community of visiting scholars, of Cambridge University lecturers and professors, and members of the University engaged primarily in research, providing an opportunity to encourage and benefit from international exchange. By 1984, when Clare Hall received its own Royal Charter, its visiting fellowship programme had become the largest of any Cambridge college; during 2007 it had more than 70 visiting fellows, mostly from overseas, and 150 graduate students.

89 Clare Hall
(photo by Chris McLeod)

Clare Hall lies on Herschel Road, adjoining Grange Road near the University Library, and features buildings designed by the distinguished Sweden-based British architect Ralph Erskine.

Map A8

(west of)

90 Robinson College
(photo by Ian Hart)

Robinson College

On Grange Road west of the University Library, Robinson (1977) is the newest of the Cambridge colleges, and the first foundation since Downing to have been set up with a massive donation from a single benefactor. A reclusive businessman who first made money selling bicycles in Bedford, David Robinson gave a total of £17m to finance a scheme which is, amongst other things, a distinct architectural success. Two tall ranges in Dorset multi-coloured brick form an inverted 'L' flanking the eastern and south-eastern ends of a large garden with woods, brook and a purpose-built open-air theatre, overlooked by rows of balconies. Between the tiered elevations runs the main college walkway, from which access is gained to a striking chapel with stained glass and furnishings by the well-known English artist John Piper. The chapel also contains a particularly fine Frobenius organ.

On the day of opening by The Queen in 1981, Sir David Robinson supplemented his original donations with a further gift, but, increasingly immobile in his old age, was unable to attend the ceremony. He died in 1987. A noted philanthropist, Robinson also funded (and named after his mother) the Rosie Maternity Hospital on Cambridge's New Addenbrooke's site on Hills Road.

University Library

Collections of books for common access have existed in the University since the 1300s, and in 1438 the first library room opened in the Old Schools, a site the University Library would occupy for nearly 500 years until it outgrew even the Cockerell Building there and moved, in 1934, into a massive purpose-built structure between Queen's Road and Grange Road. The architect of the new library was Giles Gilbert Scott, who designed Britain's old red telephone boxes to which the shape of the library tower has been likened, as well as Battersea Power Station. This is

91 Cambridge University Library

one of Britain's five legal deposit libraries, meaning that it has the right to claim a free copy of everything published in the U.K. With over 500 books arriving every working day, Cambridge University Library contains one of the largest and finest collections of books and manuscripts in the world; it is the largest open access library in Europe, containing 8 million volumes on 170 kilometres of shelving. It also provides tens of thousands of electronic journals, databases and e-books. Since 1998 the 'U.L.' has spent £30m on extensions and alterations, in the same style as Gilbert Scott's, to provide new reading rooms for manuscripts, rare books and the East Asian collections, digital resource areas, large new storage areas, better preservation facilities, and a new exhibition centre open to the public. The library's immense holdings are consulted by thousands of international scholars each year and its catalogues can be consulted freely via the Internet. Researchers who are not members of the University may apply to use the Library.

Map A4

(west of)

92 Betty and Gordon Moore Library

Centre for Mathematical Sciences

On Clarkson Road (off the northern end of Grange Road), the Centre for Mathematical Sciences brings together the University's two mathematics departments and the Isaac Newton Institute, an advanced study centre where mathematicians and scientists from around the world can pursue research projects. The Institute was opened in 1992 and named after

Cambridge's greatest scientific thinker, born 350 years earlier. In 2001 the Betty and Gordon Moore Library for the Physical Sciences, Mathematics and Technology, a branch of the University Library, was opened on the site, and the adjacent award-winning buildings, all master-minded by architect Edward Cullinan, were completed in 2002-3.

Map C4

Westminster College

Back nearer the city centre, Westminster is the United Reformed Church's theological college, set up in Cambridge in 1899 as a Presbyterian centre, on the corner where Madingley Road meets Northampton Street. Its warm brick and stone make an attractive façade, rising above a stony concourse behind high railings where the road bends. A former Cambridge theological college, Cheshunt, joined with Westminster on this site in 1967.

Map C4

Lucy Cavendish College

In a garden setting just to the west, Britain's first University college for mature women (aged 21 and over) is accommodated in a blend of Victorian and modern buildings. Lucy Cavendish College is authorised to employ only women academics, to help redress the balance of women to men in higher education. Opened in 1965, the college now has about 200 students (two-thirds at undergraduate level). Lucy Cavendish (1841-1925), daughter-in-law of the founder of the Cavendish Laboratory, was an advocate of women's education. A new library building was completed in 1999.

Map B2

St Edmund's College

On nearby Mount Pleasant stand buildings opened for the accommodation of Roman Catholic students in 1896 and converted into a postgraduate college in 1965. The name (until 1986 St Edmund's House) commemorates not the well-known patron saint of East Anglia but the thirteenth-century Edmund of Abingdon who became Archbishop of Canterbury. With a complement of 325 students (who need not nowadays be Catholic), this remains the only college in the University with a Roman Catholic chapel. Modern extensions include the street-facing tower (1992), a structure which draws on different architectural idioms and is topped by the highest room in any Cambridge college, plus new accommodation and library buildings (variously completed between 2001 and 2007).

Churchill College

Churchill College was founded in 1960, as the National and Commonwealth Memorial to Sir Winston Churchill. It is located half a mile up Madingley Road to the west, on a scale unsurpassed except by the larger of the older colleges. Although Sir Winston did not go to university, his interests are reflected in the initiative, inspired by the Massachusetts Institute of Technology, to set up a college with a primarily science and technology base. The college has, uniquely, a 70:30 ratio of science to arts students; an unusually high proportion of postgraduates; and a vigorous programme of overseas visiting fellowships. Always committed to modernity, Churchill boasts the first flats in Cambridge designed for married postgraduates, sculptures by Barbara Hepworth, Lynn Chadwick and others, and the distinction of being the first undergraduate college to decide to become co-residential. Sir Winston's papers inaugurated an archive of political, scientific and military records in the Archives Centre of the College. Those of Margaret Thatcher were added in 2003 – the first time papers of a British Prime Minister had been released during their lifetime – and approaching 600 collections are now accessible there for education and research. In 1992 The Møller Centre was opened at the college; the gift of The A.P. Møller and Chastine Mc-Kinney Møller Foundation, designed by the Danish architect Henning Larsen, it is available for hire as a dedicated residential executive education and conference centre.

93 Churchill's Møller Centre

West Cambridge Site

On the south side of Madingley Road, out beyond Churchill College, the West Cambridge Site has seen much development in recent years. It houses the Cavendish Laboratory (to which the University's Department of Physics moved from its famous predecessor in Free School Lane) as well as the Department of Veterinary Medicine and Queen's Veterinary School Hospital (which form one of the U.K.'s seven veterinary schools) and the Whittle Engineering Laboratory; but these have now been joined by the Centre for the Physics of Medicine, the Centre for Advanced Photonics and Electronics, the Nanoscience Centre, and the Computer Laboratory, with more building under way.

Cambridge has played a major role in the history of computing. Charles Babbage, Lucasian Professor of Mathematics here, had his first ideas for a calculating machine, based on the notion that machinery could be made to perform repetitive computations, before 1820, and he pursued them until his death in 1871. It was in 1949 that Maurice

94 Centre for
Advanced Photonics
and Electronics

Wilkes, head of the Cambridge department, unveiled EDSAC (Electronic Delay Storage Automatic Computer), the world's first complete and fully operational regular electronic digital stored program computer: see also p.66. The University has remained at the forefront of the practical application of computing and software engineering, as evidenced by its collaboration with Microsoft. The West Cambridge Site houses the European headquarters of Microsoft Research; and it was Wilkes who opened the William Gates Building, where the Computer Laboratory moved from its original home in Free School Lane in 2002. Gates Cambridge Scholarships, funding graduate students particularly from the U.S.A., were inaugurated in 2000 by the philanthropic Bill and Melinda Gates Foundation.

Further along the road at High Cross may be seen other important centres attracted to Cambridge partly because of the University: the building of Schlumberger Cambridge Research; and the headquarters of the British Antarctic Survey.

The large wedge of land between the Madingley Road, Huntingdon Road and M11 is due for further major development by the University as it expands over the next decades.

Madingley Rise (Observatories Site)

Map A3
(west of)

On gentle slopes to the north of Madingley Road, the grand early-nineteenth-century neo-classical architecture of the observatories still forms the centre of astronomical science in Cambridge, housing the

95 Telescope on the Observatories Site

University's Institute of Astronomy. The Northumberland 12-inch refracting telescope is in the largest of the domes. This was briefly the world's biggest telescope: in 1846 James Challis used it in a systematic search for the planet that became known as Neptune, based on calculations by John Couch Adams who succeeded Challis as director of the Cambridge Observatory (the first observation of Neptune was however to be from Berlin, later in 1846). Strong traditions of theoretical and radio astronomy in the University – for which Antony Hewish and Martin Ryle won the Nobel Prize for Physics in 1974 – attracted the Royal Greenwich Observatory here for eight years between 1990 and 1998, until its closure and re-integration as part of Greenwich's National Maritime Museum.

In the eighteenth century many of the Cambridge colleges had their own observatories, with telescopes mounted on the top of chapels and gatehouses. The Madingley Rise site now hosts public observing nights throughout the winter, when the Northumberland and other telescopes may be used, their observations beamed via digital projectors to screens around the grounds.

Further afield, the University's Mullard Radio Astronomy Observatory may also be seen, from the A603 beyond Barton four miles south-west of Cambridge, its array of radio telescopes following the course of the old railway line to Oxford, which provided a site that was conveniently straight and flat. Neutron stars were discovered here in 1967.

American Cemetery

Map A3

(west of)

Though on former University land, the American Cemetery (near Madingley, three miles west of Cambridge) is not part of the University. Its chapel and hillside site attract transatlantic visitors, as a memorial to countless American servicemen who died in Europe during the Second World War, many of them from the numerous air force bases scattered across East Anglia.

Madingley Hall

Map A3

(west of)

The University's Institute of Continuing Education has its headquarters in a Tudor mansion in rolling countryside above Madingley village. Here well-attended residential courses are organised throughout the year, all open for enrolment to members of the public. The gateway (c.1470) leading to the old stables yard is that which stood at the front of the east front of the Old Schools until Stephen Wright's reconstruction of the 1750s.

96 American Cemetery

97 Girton gate tower

Girton College

No women's college existed in Cambridge or Oxford when in 1869 educational reformer Emily Davies set up a female establishment, on the Cambridge collegiate model, in Hitchin, Hertfordshire, to prepare students for the Cambridge tripos. The spirit of reform was strong, and by the time she moved in 1873 to a spacious site on the edge of Girton village, two and a half miles north-west of the city, a women's college (the forerunner of Newnham) had already been founded in Cambridge. Change occurred slowly and Girton received its formal college charter in 1924. Until the second half of the twentieth century it and Newnham remained the only two female colleges in a University that continued to be dominated by men.

Girton is a showpiece of 1870s red-brick architecture by the prolific Alfred Waterhouse. Its tower, turrets and gables are visible against the lush fields on the north-western approach to the city. Following the co-educational reforms of the 1960s and '70s Girton admitted men (1979), who now account for half of its student numbers, making this one of the larger colleges at first-degree level, with over 500 undergraduates (as well as 200 or more postgraduates). Uniquely among Cambridge colleges, the fellowship of Girton is evenly balanced between women and men.

In 2005 Girton completed its new library and archive, for which it has received national awards, accommodating the documents amassed from its pioneering role in the history of women's education.

Map A1
(north-west of)

Ascension Parish Burial Ground

If you are someone who enjoys a contemplative browsing of gravestones, this secluded churchyard is a must. Accessible via a lane leading off Huntingdon Road just north-west of Storey's Way, it provided a final resting-place for many of Cambridge's great and good. Graves include those of Ludwig Wittgenstein, G. E. Moore, A. C. Benson, John Cockcroft, Frances Cornford, W. W. Skeat, John Couch Adams, Alfred Marshall and several members of the Darwin family. A plaque near the chapel provides a guide to the graves.

Map A1

Fitzwilliam College

The origins of this modern college go back to the formation of the Non-Collegiate Students' Board in 1869. The Board's headquarters were established at 31 and 32 Trumpington Street, near the Fitzwilliam Museum, and became known in 1887 as Fitzwilliam Hall and in 1924 as Fitzwilliam House. When full collegiate status was gained in 1966, the college moved to its present site on Huntingdon Road, on the way out towards Girton.

The highlights of Fitzwilliam's modernist architecture are the dining hall by Denys Lasdun, with its unusual lantern of hooded arches and high, clear glass windows; the internationally acclaimed chapel by Richard MacCormac, who also built New Court; and Gatehouse Court, designed to provide a new entrance to the college in 2004. A Victorian house, The Grove, has been sympathetically incorporated into the eight-acre grounds. In 2008, during an archaeological dig in preparation for new library buildings, the first Bronze Age relics to be found in the city of Cambridge were unearthed here.

Map B1

New Hall

Near the city side of Fitzwilliam lies New Hall, founded in 1954 to provide more places for women in the University. The college remains committed to ensuring a high-quality education for women of all backgrounds, with some 450 students (all female) and a mixed male-female fellowship of around 50. Its current site was developed in 1962-4 on land originally occupied and then donated by descendants of Charles Darwin. Of special note are the elegantly articulated dome of the dining hall and the fine library with its vaulted roof (both forming the centre of Fountain Court), and the landscaped grounds including the 'Transit of Venus' garden which won a Bronze Medal at the 2007

98 New Hall's
Kaetsu Centre

Chelsea Flower Show. Donations of around 300 paintings and sculptures by leading women artists have created a collection unique in Britain, and this is open for display. The college houses the Kaetsu Educational and Cultural Centre, built in collaboration with one of Japan's oldest foundations for the education of women. New Hall provided the first woman Vice-Chancellor of the University, Rosemary Murray (also the college's first President, after whom the library is named), as well as the University's first woman Treasurer, Joanna Womack.

Map H2

Jesus Green and River Cam

Along Chesterton Lane a footbridge leads to Jesus Green, a public recreational area which is an ideal starting-point for river walks. Here a Protestant martyr, John Hullier of King's College, was burned at the stake for his faith in the mid-sixteenth century; and here in the nineteenth century plans were made (but never fulfilled) to build a railway station. A weir lies on the Cam, and further east there is an outdoor swimming pool.

Visitors with more time should strike out along the river path, under the Victoria Road bridge, and on across Midsummer Common

99 The 'Bumps' on the River Cam

and Stourbridge Common, where an annual fair took place for more than 500 years from the early 1200s, attracting traders and theatrical entertainers from all over Europe in Elizabethan times and becoming the largest gathering of its kind in Europe. On the north bank the college boathouses are feverish with activity early in the mornings during term, as rowers limber up and gather their oars. At most times of the year it is possible to see boat crews in training on this stretch of river, and indeed all the way down to Chesterton and Baits Bite Lock a few miles away, where the annual 'Lents' and 'May Bumps' (intercollegiate rowing competitions) take place. Rowing is the best known of many sports pursued at a high level by Cambridge University students, some of whom will win a Blue by competing in their chosen sport against Oxford. A select few rowers make it into the Boat Race, the annual contest with Oxford on the River Thames in London, which continues to compel worldwide interest.

Map I1

(north of)

Science Park

In the 1980s the University and colleges helped fund Cambridge's expansion as an international centre of technological development, and the Science Park, founded by Trinity College in 1970 as the first of its kind in the country, provides thriving testimony to this impetus: a place where academia and industry meet. It and the nearby Innovation Park lie two and a half miles north of the city where the A1309/A10 Ely road reaches the A14 bypass. The monumental NAPP Laboratories (1981-3), with their huge white frames and glass fronts, are imposingly visible from the road. Computer and pharmaceutical companies are among the 90 or more businesses which make this high-tech industrial estate, retaining close research links with the University, an ongoing success.

Map I9

(east of)

Hughes Hall

Located a mile to the east of the city centre overlooking Fenner's, the University cricket ground, Hughes Hall began in 1885 as the Cambridge Training College for Women Teachers. It moved in 1895 into new red-brick buildings reminiscent of those at Newnham (the college which helped set it up) and in 1949 changed its name in commemoration of Miss E. P. Hughes, its first Principal. Men were first admitted in 1973 to read for higher degrees and diplomas, when Hughes Hall became a graduate college of the University. A residential and dining range, built on a curve around the northern boundary of the cricket pitch, was opened in 2005.

Map I12

Scott Polar Research Institute and Tennis Court Road area

On Lensfield Road, west of the Catholic church, an institute named after Captain Robert Falcon Scott, the British explorer who died having reached the South Pole in 1912, is devoted to research relating to the polar regions. Established in 1920 and now housed in a building of 1934, the Institute includes a public museum featuring exhibits of Arctic and Antarctic exploration. Letters discovered with the bodies of the ill-fated explorers of 1912 (including Dr Edward Wilson, a Cambridge graduate) are on display. The statue in the garden was cast by Scott's widow Kathleen. In 1998 a new library was opened at the Institute, which is also home to the International Glaciological Society, the Scientific Committee on Antarctic Research, and the World Data Centre for Glaciology (Cambridge), as well as forming part of the NERC Centre for Polar Observation and Modelling.

Alongside, the University's Department of Chemistry (built 1953-60) is a major centre for Organic and Inorganic Chemistry inspired by Lord Todd, winner of the Nobel Prize in 1957. The Chemistry Library with its pyramidical light well, part of the Unilever Centre for Molecular Informatics, was opened in 2001.

Nearby, Tennis Court Road heads north towards the Downing Site. Along this street we find, on the west side, the Department of Pharmacology, Institute of Biotechnology, Wellcome Trust Centre for Stem Cell Research (opened in 2006), Cambridge Systems Biology Centre, and the Gurdon Institute (opened in 2005 and devoted to research into cancer and developmental biology). Here too is the Department of Biochemistry, which has, with the Medical Research Council's Cambridge laboratories, been responsible for leading research projects in the biochemical field, impelled by the work done in Cambridge on proteins and nucleic acids by Fred Sanger, the first person to win two Nobel Prizes for Chemistry (in 1958 and 1980). At the northern end of the road, Pembroke College has recently added its Foundress Court, with a prominent sundial carved directly into the stone.

Map 110

(south-east of)

100 Homerton's tower in springtime

(photo courtesy of Homerton College)

Homerton College

Homerton has been an approved society of the University since 1977. Founded as an Academy in London in 1768, with roots stretching back to 1695, it moved to Cambridge in 1895, into the striking neo-Tudor red-brick buildings (by Giles and Gough) which housed the former Cavendish College. An ambitious scheme of new building was undertaken in the early 2000s around the south-facing Victorian and Edwardian core, providing excellent accommodation for undergraduates and graduates, together with conference facilities, within spacious and beautifully maintained lawns and gardens. Alongside the college are the impressive new Faculty of Education buildings (2005).

Following its move to Cambridge, Homerton soon became recognized as a top-ranking teacher-training institution, producing many generations of students with a reputation for high academic standards combined with strong practical teaching skills. In 1999 and 2000, Homerton topped the national league table as the best overall provider of teacher training. While the college, now mixed, continues to maintain strong links with Education, in 2001 it began a carefully planned process of academic diversification. Its fellowship has expanded steadily, and it now admits undergraduates to almost all other Cambridge triposes, in addition to recruiting a substantial number of graduates studying at master's and doctoral level. Homerton is currently the largest college in Cambridge in terms of overall student numbers, with around 1,100 students.

Map 110
(south-east of)

Addenbrooke's Hospital

One of the country's foremost teaching and research hospitals, and among the largest hospital complexes in Europe, Addenbrooke's houses the University's School of Clinical Medicine, and has led the way in many medical developments of recent years. It was founded in the mid-eighteenth century with £4,767 left by Dr John Addenbrooke, the first Englishman to bequeath his private fortune for a voluntary hospital (see pp.61-2 for the original site). Addenbrooke's now treats over half a million patients each year and continues to expand. In 2007 The Queen opened the Cancer Research UK Cambridge Research Institute within the Li Ka Shing Centre.

Map 112
(south-east of)

Cambridge University Press

101 Edinburgh Building
(photo by Marc Anderson)

The prominent brown building seen from the London train just before arrival at Cambridge railway station is the principal warehouse of the University Press (see also pp.26-7 and 49-50), part of its Edinburgh Building complex which opened in 1981. The printing factory had already been established on the same Shaftesbury Road site in 1963. One of the largest on-site storage facilities of any publisher in the world, the warehouse contains c.10 million books and CDs.

Map 113
(south of)

Botanic Garden

The University Botanic Garden presents a beautiful series of landscapes a mile south of the city centre. This historic site was set up in 1831 by John Henslow, Darwin's guiding light, as the plant collection for research and teaching in the University. Replacing a much smaller garden established in 1762 where the New Museums Site now is, it uniquely combines the science of plants with superb horticulture and brilliant plantings.

Henslow's founding vision of a Botanic Garden for everyone to enjoy and benefit from has continued to this day. The Garden has an internationally important collection of 8,000 species developed around a framework of mature trees. Within this setting is the intricate pattern of 150 beds making up the Systematic Beds, the majestic rock garden rising above the lake, and a series of themed plantings including the winter garden, woodland garden and dry garden. The huge teak glasshouse

102 Botanic Garden

range has recently been restored to its former splendour, presenting the world's flora through the Drama of Diversity display.

Map B13

(south of)

Grantchester Meadows

The Meadows are best accessed via Grantchester Street, which leaves the Barton Road at the south-west corner of Lammas Land. From there a one-and-a-half-mile walk takes you to the village of Grantchester. You can leave the main path and wander along the riverbank, an idyllic setting where punt-parties stop for picnics. Rock group Pink Floyd hail from Cambridge and their guitarist Dave Gilmour was born on the street named Grantchester Meadows. He and Syd Barrett, a school friend of Roger Waters (who wrote and performed a song about the Meadows on Floyd's album *Ummagumma*), attended the Cambridgeshire College of Arts & Technology, now Anglia Ruskin University.

Wolfson College

While the other foundations of the 1960s were spawned with support from existing colleges or non-University sources, the college on Barton Road, to the south west beyond Newnham, was established by the University itself in 1965. Financial independence was achieved by the fledgling 'University College' on 1 January 1973 when the Wolfson Foundation (created by Scottish philanthropist Isaac Wolfson) provided it with £2m and a new name. Its modern buildings form an 'E' shape on a thoughtfully laid-out site. Further significant expansion took place with the opening of the Lee Library (named after its benefactor, Dr S. T. Lee of Singapore) in 1994, and new student rooms were built on the western side of the site in the 1990s, culminating in the opening of the Chancellor's Centre of Graduate Studies in 2005. This latter building houses the University's statue of Prince Albert (Chancellor, 1847-61) by John Henry Foley. Though begun as a postgraduate institution, Wolfson now gives c.15%-20% of its places to undergraduates – but maintains a minimum entry age of 21. With over two-thirds of its students coming regularly from outside the U.K., the college claims to be the most cosmopolitan in Cambridge.

103 Cambridge spring blossom

104 Punters at
Garret Hostel Bridge

Glossary

There follows a list, with brief explanations, of University-related terms. The booklet *University of Cambridge: The Way it Works* (second edition, 2006), available from the University Offices (the 'Old Schools'), or the Office of External Affairs and Communications, or online at www.cam.ac.uk, is gratefully acknowledged as a source for much of this information. The book *Bedders, Bulldogs and Bedells: A Cambridge Glossary*, listed in the 'Further reading' section, provides entertaining definitions of many additional University words and phrases.

An asterisk* indicates a term defined elsewhere in the Glossary.

Academical Year This extends from 1 October to 30 September, and is divided into three Terms* (Michaelmas, Lent and Easter) and three vacations.

Admission Undergraduate students are selected and admitted by the colleges, through the agency of the Cambridge Admissions Office. Graduate students apply through the Board of Graduate Studies, which also helps to arrange admission to a college.

Appointments Committees Autonomous standing committees, whose duty is to make appointments to most University offices except professorships and readerships. They conduct their business according to strict procedural rules. These committees make substantive appointments, subject to confirmation of salary and similar details by the Council* or General Board*.

Arms The Arms of the University of Cambridge were granted in 1573 and consist of a white cross with black ermine 'tails' and a clasped book in the middle, between four lions in the 'passant gardant' position (walking but with one leg raised and facing the observer): see p.12.

B.A. The B.A., or Bachelor of Arts, is the name of the primary degree obtained by most Cambridge University students after successfully completing their undergraduate course of study and tripos* examinations in the University. Cambridge students reading Medicine or Veterinary Medicine take a B.A. in an appropriate subject and then pursue an extended course of study leading to e.g. the M.B. (Bachelor of Medicine), B.Chir. (Bachelor of Surgery), or Vet. M.B. (Bachelor of Veterinary Medicine); and there are also Bachelors' degrees in Divinity and Music. See also M.A.* and Doctorate*.

Backs The Backs is the name given to the kilometre-long stretch of riverbank and adjoining college grounds running from Darwin College in the south to Magdalene College in the north.

Ballot A poll of the Regent House* (or very occasionally the Senate*) on a motion put before it. A ballot of the Regent House takes place if called for by the Council* or by 25 members of the Regent House, and is conducted by post under prescribed rules of procedure.

Bedell See Esquire Bedells*.

Blue Anyone competing for Cambridge against the University of Oxford in one of a range of particular sports may be awarded a Blue, which includes the entitlement to wear a special blazer in the Cambridge sky-blue colour. Some sports merit a Half-Blue rather than the full award, meaning that the blazer must be tempered with buff. Cambridge's distinctive colour is thought to originate in the Boat Race against Oxford of 1836, when the Cambridge boat, lacking proper colours at its bow, was decorated in a makeshift ribbon which happened to be sky-blue. Annual sporting contests between the two universities are known as Varsity Matches.

Board of Scrutiny A review body consisting of the two Proctors*, the two Pro-Proctors, and eight members elected from the Regent House*. Its function is to act on behalf of the Regent House by scrutinising the accounts of the University, the Annual Report of the Council* and the General Board*, and the University budget.

Cantab The word used to indicate that a degree* was earned at Cambridge. It is an abbreviation of Cantabrigiensis, the adjectival form of the Latinised name of the city, Cantabrigia.

Central Bodies The collective term for the Council* and the General Board of the Faculties*, and their committees.

Chancellor The Duke of Edinburgh has, since 1977, filled the role of constitutional head of the University of Cambridge. As Chancellor, elected by the Senate*, he has certain statutory duties, his principal public responsibility in modern times being the conferment of Honorary Degrees*.

Coat of Arms See Arms*.

College Readers are referred to pp.3-4 for a discussion of what a college is and how it functions within, and in relation to, the public University.

Congregation A meeting of the Regent House* for the formal conduct of certain items of University business, principally the conferment of degrees*. Congregations take place in the Senate-House regularly throughout the year. Special Congregations take place from time to time for the conferment of Honorary Degrees*, and three days at the end of the Easter Term are reserved for the graduation of most first-degree students

(General Admission*). The Vice-Chancellor* or a deputy presides at Congregations, unless the Chancellor* is present. A Congregation is also held at the beginning of each academical year* for the election of the Proctors* and their deputies. Immediately prior to this, the Vice-Chancellor gives an address to the University.

Council A chiefly elected body that is the University's principal executive and policy-making committee. It is one of the two central bodies (the other is the General Board of the Faculties*) and has responsibility for the business of the University in its broader aspect, except that relating directly to its teaching and research programme. It is the formal link between the University and the colleges, has overall responsibility for planning and resource allocation, conducts negotiations with external bodies, and is concerned with student affairs, apart from admissions and teaching.

The Council is also responsible through its Finance Committee for accounting, budgeting, and control of investments, and for the management of property. The Council has in most cases the responsibility of presenting to the Regent House* business that requires its assent. The Council generally meets monthly except in August, with the Vice-Chancellor* as Chairman and the Registrary* as Secretary.

Court A Cambridge court is an inner yard, usually surrounded on three or more sides by buildings, found within the colleges, the Old Schools (see p.23-4), etc. In Cambridge, the Oxford equivalent term of 'quadrangle' is never used.

Crest of the University See Arms*.

Dean The Dean of a college is usually the fellow*, generally an ordained priest, with responsibility for the college chapel and its services, although in some colleges the title is used of the official responsible for internal discipline. Many colleges also have a Chaplain, who serves under the Dean. Only in the Faculties of Medicine and Veterinary Medicine is the term Dean used to indicate an academic office.

Degree The qualification awarded after a course of study and examinations (see Tripos*) or for other reasons. There are various types of Cambridge degree: see B.A.*, Doctorate*, Honorary Degree*, M.A.*.

Department A department is a subdivision of a University faculty*, more common in science than in arts subjects. There are about 60 departments in the University.

Director of Studies A Director of Studies is appointed by a college to advise on and oversee the work of students in that college taking a particular subject, including advice on examinations and lectures, and for the assignment of the student to one or more Supervisors*. The term Tutor* is not used in Cambridge in this connection.

Discussions
Meetings of members of the University, held on certain Tuesdays in Term*, at which business put forward by the Council* or other bodies in the form of Reports* may be commented upon by any member of the Regent House*, the Senate or any other member of the University including students. The proceedings are usually formal rather than spontaneous. It is sometimes the case that a representative of the body that originated the business will be present to speak in defence of the Report. The Vice-Chancellor*, or a deputy, presides. The body that originated the Report subsequently advises the Council on a response (or Notice) to the remarks made, prior to the proposal of any Grace*.

Doctorate
A doctorate is the degree of doctor, most often in Cambridge a Ph.D. (i.e. Doctorate of Philosophy). This is a senior degree, higher than the B.A.* or M.A.*, and is usually achieved after three years of postgraduate study. Higher doctorates, such as the LL.D. (Doctorate of Law) or D.D. (Doctorate of Divinity) are the most senior qualifications in the University, and are usually conferred on those who have published extensive original works in their field.

Don
This old-fashioned colloquial term, now falling out of use in Cambridge, derives from the Latin word 'dominus' (lord, master, sir) and denotes any senior member of the University or of a college, including professors, lecturers, and Directors of Studies*.

Electors
A body of persons appointed (sometimes for a particular occasion, sometimes on a long-standing basis) to select a person for certain senior offices, principally professorships. The Vice-Chancellor*, or a deputy, presides. The rules of procedure resemble those for Appointments Committees*, but there are certain additional provisions (e.g. that a body of Electors must meet twice in order to make an appointment).

Emeritus/Emerita
A term applied to the Vice-Chancellor*, professors, readers, and holders of certain other senior positions, who have retired after the age of 60. In Cambridge the term is not conferred as an individual mark of distinction (although there is provision for appointment of Honorary Professors).

Esquire Bedells
Two officials whose duties are ceremonial. They have certain important responsibilities at Congregations*, and carry the University Maces before the Chancellor* or Vice-Chancellor* in processions. The Senior Esquire Bedell has a general responsibility for the correct formulation and wearing of academical dress.

Faculty
Each of Cambridge's faculties is an administrative subdivision of the University responsible for teaching and research within a particular academic subject or group of subjects. Examples are the Faculties of Asian & Middle Eastern Studies, Biology, Classics, Computer Science & Technology, Divinity, Earth Sciences & Geography, Education, English, Mathematics, Music, and Physics & Chemistry. Some of the larger faculties are divided into departments* for administrative convenience; this sub-division is less common in the arts faculties. Each faculty has an elected Faculty Board that is responsible to the General Board* for the provision of adequate teaching and facilities for research. Reports on academic matters mainly originate from the appropriate Faculty Boards.

Fellow
A fellow (who may in most colleges be male or female) is a senior member of a college, usually elected to a particular position of authority and responsibility in relation to the academic work and government of the college. The fellowship of a college might include full, research, visiting, honorary, and emeritus fellows, and fellow commoners, all with differing degrees and types of status and responsibility. Fellows often (though not necessarily) have teaching and administrative duties within the college.

Fly Sheets
Manifestos or explanations circulated by members of the Regent House* to enlarge upon issues put forward for decision by ballot*.

Fresher
Colloquial term for an undergraduate student in his or her first year.

Full Term
The academical year* is divided into three Terms* (Michaelmas, Lent and Easter). The central portion of each term, during which teaching takes place and members of the University are normally expected to be in residence, is called Full Term. It is typically eight-and-a-half weeks long.

General Admission
Three Congregations* held on successive days towards the end of June each year are termed Days of General Admission to Degrees. These are the occasions on which the majority of undergraduates who have completed their final year proceed in person to their first degree*, in most cases the degree of B.A.*. Degrees are also conferred at eight other Congregations in the course of the year.

General Board of the Faculties (the General Board)
One of the two central bodies (the other being Council*), with general responsibility for the teaching and research programme of the University. In particular the Board's duty is to advise the University on educational policy and to control the resources needed for the proper implementation of that policy. The General Board is responsible for the

113

standard of teaching and research, for the appointment of examiners, and for ensuring that the teaching officers of the University adhere to the regulations and satisfactorily perform their duties. In practice most matters to do with teaching or research are referred to the Board. The Secretary of the Board is the Academic Secretary, and the Chairman is the Vice-Chancellor*. It meets approximately every fourth Wednesday in Full Term*, with certain additional meetings. The Board has a number of important standing committees, including a Needs Committee which deals with resource allocation, an Education Committee dealing with the curriculum and the content of examinations, and a Research Policy Committee; and it has joint committees with the Council which deal with resource allocation and personnel matters.

Gowns and hoods   Undergraduates of each college have a distinctive knee-length gown, usually black (except for those at Trinity and Gonville and Caius, which are dark blue). These are worn on formal occasions including visits to the Senate-House, and to dinner and chapel (in the case of some of the colleges). A hood is worn with the gown at the graduation ceremony. M.A.* and doctorate* degrees entitle the holder to a different status of gown.

Graces   Motions put forward (normally by the Council*) for decision by the Regent House* or very occasionally by the Senate*. They may be approved without dissent if no opposition is raised within ten days. A ballot* of the Regent House on a Grace takes place if requested by the Council or 25 members of the Regent House.

Grace is also the prayer said before dinner at the more traditional colleges, and in some it is still proclaimed in Latin by a student.

Graduation   This ceremony takes place in the Senate-House about ten times a year. Graduands from each college parade together in formal dress to receive their degrees*. Special ceremonies each June, known as General Admission*, are the occasions when the majority of students receive their B.A.* degrees after three or four years of study.

High Steward   One of the high officers of the University, the High Steward may be called upon to substitute for the Chancellor* in some closely defined circumstances, for example in resolving disputes concerning the obligations of colleges to the University.

High Table   Most of the colleges preserve a formal dining arrangement, with fellows and their guests sitting together at a special table, separate from the student body. In the older halls the High Table stands at one end, at right angles to the student tables, and may be raised above them on a dais.

Honorary Degree   This is a special degree, usually at the doctorate* level, awarded to a person of great distinction, either from the U.K. or elsewhere. It is often conferred by the Chancellor* himself, at a colourful ceremony held each June. It is the highest honour that the University can bestow.

Incorporation   A procedure by which a University Officer or a fellow* of a college who is a graduate of the University of Oxford or Dublin (Trinity College) may be admitted to the corresponding Cambridge degree*.

Long Vacation   The three Terms* are separated by three vacations (Christmas, Easter and Long Vacation) during which undergraduate* teaching is suspended. During the Long Vacation, which lasts for 13 weeks, a period is set aside for certain special teaching in connection with some courses, usually now language and computer courses; this is known as the Long Vacation Period of Residence, commonly called the 'Long Vac Term'. Other University activities, especially research, continue during vacations.

M.A.   The M.A. is the Cambridge Master of Arts degree. In most U.K. universities, the Master of Arts is a degree awarded by examination. At Cambridge, the M.A. is not available as a postgraduate qualification. It is conferred by right on holders of the Bachelor's degree of the University, who become eligible for it six years after the end of their first term of residence in the University, and on certain other senior members.

Master   The Master of a college is its head, usually elected by the other fellows for a limited term, and in some cases appointed from outside. All of the colleges in the University have Masters except for Clare Hall, Hughes Hall, Lucy Cavendish, New Hall, Queens', and Wolfson, which call their heads Presidents instead; Homerton and Newnham, which have Principals; Girton, a Mistress; King's, a Provost; and Robinson, a Warden. All of these may be known colloquially as 'Heads of Houses'.

Matriculation   Although a formal University matriculation ceremony has not taken place since 1962, all new Cambridge students must still enrol or register with their college by signing a declaration that they will obey the regulations, thus formally matriculating. Most colleges hold a matriculation dinner for their new students and take a matriculation photograph. The word comes from the Latin 'matrix', meaning roll or register. 'Coming up' is a colloquial term often used in place of 'matriculating'.

Non Placet   Latin 'it does not please': originally the call made at a Congregation* by those seeking a vote on a proposal for University legislation, it is still used to describe opposition to a Grace*.

Ordinances   The University Statutes allow the University to make regulations, known as Ordinances, for the proper conduct of its affairs. Ordinances, and amendments of them, are made either by the Regent House*, the Senate* or the General Board*. Ordinances may relate to any aspect of the University's business.

Ph.D. See Doctorate*.

Porter Nearly all of the colleges have porters, who are members of the college staff with a range of responsibilities normally directed by a Head Porter. To students and visitors alike, the porter is most familiar as the figure who occupies the porters' lodge at the college entrance, answering queries, guarding the gate, handing out keys, and harbouring a fund of information about domestic arrangements within the college.

Postgraduate A postgraduate is a student with a first degree* from Cambridge or elsewhere, now studying for a higher degree.

Proctors Two officials, one designated Senior and the other Junior, who are elected annually by the Regent House* on the nomination of the colleges in rotation. They are the representatives of the Regent House in formal and disciplinary matters. They have ceremonial duties at Congregations* and elsewhere, and are responsible for maintaining public order and freedom of speech in the University. They serve on the Board of Scrutiny* together with the Pro-Proctors. The Junior Proctor has particular responsibilities in relation to Student Union matters and University societies. A person nominated as Proctor usually serves first for one year as Pro-Proctor, then for a year as Proctor and finally for a further year as Deputy Proctor.

Punt In Cambridge or Oxford, punters are people who propel or ride in the long, flat boats that can be seen on the river at virtually any time of the year and, during Term, at most times of the day or night. There are public punt-hire stations at the Mill Pond (Granta Place), Quayside (Magdalene Bridge), and elsewhere. Chauffeurs may also be hired. Pleasure punting of this kind developed in the late nineteenth century, in boats based on fishing and cargo vessels used in earlier years to navigate the shallow waters of the Thames Valley. The trend reached Cambridge in about 1902 and is now, in spite of its widespread national popularity during the Edwardian years, almost exclusively a Cambridge or Oxford pursuit.

Regent House The Regent House is the governing body of the University, comprising about 4,000 members who are teaching and administrative officers from the University and colleges. The Regent House is the legislative authority of the University and the body to which proposals for significant changes in procedures or policies must be referred for assent. When such a decision is required, the matter is presented in the form of a Grace* published by the Council* in the Reporter*. If a proposal is controversial the Regent House may be required to decide by voting on the proposal in a postal ballot. The Regent House is also the principal electoral body, elects most members of the Council and the Board of Scrutiny*, and makes appointments by Grace.

Registrary The principal administrative officer of the University and the head of the Unified Administrative Service.

Reporter The University's official journal, containing University business, appointments, vacancies, events, Reports*, Graces*, and reports of Discussions*. The Reporter is published weekly on Wednesdays in Term, and occasionally in vacations. A special edition ('the Officers' number') published at the start of the Michaelmas Term contains full details of the membership of all official committees, boards, etc., and a full list of substantive University academic and administrative appointments. There are other special issues, for instance dealing with admission statistics, University accounts, and examination results.

Reports Reasoned arguments put to the University in support of certain changes or innovations, the proposals being published in the Reporter*, discussed, and, if necessary, voted upon in a ballot*.

Residence Most students and academic staff are required to be in residence during each period of Full Term*; unless specially exempted, staff and students must live within a prescribed radius of Great St Mary's Church. Students may not generally proceed to their degrees* unless their colleges certify that they have 'kept terms' by being in residence for the specified period.

Scarlet Days Days on which holders of Cambridge Doctorate* degrees are required to wear in public their festal or scarlet gowns*. The permanent list of such days is defined by Ordinance*, but in addition the Vice-Chancellor* may prescribe other days as Scarlet Days, if they are occasions for instance of national rejoicing or celebration, or of other special importance to the University.

School Administrative grouping of faculties* and other institutions. A School's responsibilities are concerned mainly with distribution of resources to its constituent institutions. There are six Schools (Arts & Humanities, Biological Sciences, Clinical Medicine, Humanities & Social Sciences, Physical Sciences, and Technology). The word School is also sometimes used to describe a building and the studies carried out in it, or as a familiar title for certain faculties.

Senate Holders of Cambridge degrees at M.A.* level or higher comprise the University Senate. Until 1926 the Senate was the governing body of the University (a role now played by the Regent House*). It elects the Chancellor* and the High Steward*, and membership confers senior status and certain privileges such as borrowing books from the University Library.

Septemviri A University court with seven members; it is the ultimate court of appeal in relation to disciplinary offences.

Shield of the University See Arms*.

Statute The University of Cambridge is governed by a framework of statutes drawn up in 1926 and based on a constitutional code dating from the thirteenth century. Amendments (of which there have been many since 1926) require the approval of The Queen in Council. The University is a common law corporation.

Supervisor A college teacher, who teaches undergraduates*, either individually or in small groups, in his or her subject.

Syndicate A committee set up to oversee a particular function or activity within the University, sometimes academic and sometimes administrative. It includes senior members of the University drawn from various areas. Examples are the Accommodation Syndicate, Library Syndicate, Press Syndicate and Sports Syndicate. It has also been the practice to appoint occasional syndicates to advise on major particular questions of current importance, and this is still done from time to time.

Term The academical year* is divided into three Terms (Michaelmas: October to December; Lent: January to March; and Easter: April to June). See also Full Term* (which is a smaller part of each Term), Long Vacation* and Residence*.

Tripos This is the name given to a Cambridge examination leading to the B.A. degree*. The word derives from the Greco-Latin for a 'three-legged stool' and refers to the object on which the examiner used to sit while listening to candidates offering oral defences of their work before the introduction of written examinations. Unique to Cambridge, this sense of the word has been in use here since at least the sixteenth century.

Tripos results are graded into the classes of 'First' (the highest result, usually obtained by c.20% of students), '2:1' (c.52%), '2:2' (c.23%) and 'Third' (c.5%).

Tutor A college officer responsible for the welfare and guidance of a group of undergraduates, but not, in Cambridge, for their academic instruction which is carried out by their Director of Studies*.

Undergraduate   An undergraduate is a student studying for a first degree*, normally the B.A.*. Most Cambridge undergraduates are in their late teens or early twenties, but there are also mature students who matriculate* at a later age.

Vacation   See Long Vacation*.

Vice-Chancellor   The Vice-Chancellor oversees the administration of the University and is its principal full-time resident officer, with a number of important ceremonial and statutory duties. He or she is appointed by the Regent House* on the nomination of the Council* for a period of up to seven years. There are also five salaried Pro-Vice-Chancellors with defined responsibilities and a number of Deputy Vice-Chancellors who are appointed by the Vice-Chancellor to act on formal occasions such as Congregations* and to undertake particular duties.

Further reading

For more detailed discussions of Cambridge's architecture, the reader is referred to *The Buildings of England: Cambridgeshire*, by Nikolaus Pevsner (Penguin Books, 1954; second edition, 1970, now published by Yale University Press), *Cambridge Architecture*, by Tim Rawle (Trefoil Books, 1985; second edition André Deutsch Limited, 1993), and the works by Nicholas Ray and Willis & Clark listed below. What follows is a selection of useful books on Cambridge published by Cambridge University Press, all available from the Press's bookshop at 1 Trinity Street (see p.26-7).

The Story of Cambridge, by Stephanie Boyd, 2005.

Cambridge Architecture: A Concise Guide, by Nicholas Ray, 1994.

The Architectural History of the University of Cambridge: Volumes I, II, and III, by Robert Willis and John Willis Clark,1886; reissued 1988.

A Concise History of the University of Cambridge, by Elisabeth Leedham-Green, 1996.

A History of the University of Cambridge:
  Volume I: The University to 1546, by Damien Riehl Leader, 1989;
  Volume II: 1546-1750, by Victor Morgan and Christopher Brooke, 2004;
  Volume III: 1750-1870, by Peter Searby, 1997;
  Volume IV: 1870-1990, by Christopher Brooke, 1992.

A History of Cambridge University Press, by D. J. McKitterick:
  Volume I: Printing and the Book Trade in Cambridge, 1534-1698, 1992;
  Volume 2: Scholarship and Commerce, 1698-1872, 1998;
  Volume 3: New Worlds for Learning, 1873-1972, 2004.

Cambridge University Press 1584-1984, by M. H. Black, 1984.

A Short History of Cambridge University Press, by M. H. Black, 1992; second edition, 2000.

University of Cambridge Official Map; fourth edition, 2006.
Bedders, Bulldogs and Bedells: A Cambridge Glossary, by Frank Stubbings, 1995.

Cambridge Street-Names: Their Origins and Associations, by Ronald Gray, Derek Stubbings and Virén Sahai, 2000.

Cambridge Contributions, edited by Sarah J. Ormrod, 1998.

Cambridge Minds, edited by Richard Mason, 1994.

Cambridge Scientific Minds, edited by Peter Harman and Simon Mitton, 2002.

Cambridge Women: Twelve Portraits, edited by Edward Shils and Carmen Blacker, 1996.

Women at Cambridge, by Rita McWilliams Tullberg, 1998.

Cambridge Theatres: College, University and Town Stages, 1464-1720, by Alan H. Nelson, 1994.

Cambridge in the Age of the Enlightenment: Science, Religion and Politics from the Restoration to the French Revolution, by John Gascoigne, 1989.

The Cambridge Apostles, 1820-1914: Liberalism, Imagination, and Friendship in British Intellectual and Professional Life, by W. C. Lubenow, 1998.

Printing and Publishing for the University of Cambridge: Three Hundred Years of the Press Syndicate, by Gordon Johnson, 1999.

The Making of the Wren Library: Trinity College, Cambridge, by D. J. McKitterick, 1995.

Lady Margaret Beaufort and her Professors of Divinity at Cambridge: 1502 to 1649, by Patrick Collinson, Richard Rex and Graham Stanton, 2003.

The Whipple Museum of the History of Science: Instruments and Interpretations, to Celebrate the 60th Anniversary of R. S. Whipple's Gift to the University of Cambridge, edited by Liba Taub and Frances Willmoth, 2006.

Examining the World: A History of the University of Cambridge Local Examinations Syndicate, edited by Sandra Raban, 2008.

University Politics: F. M. Cornford's Cambridge and his Advice to the Young Academic Politician, by Gordon Johnson, 1994; second edition, 2008.

Cambridge University Historical Register Supplements (historical lists of University members).

The University of Cambridge Statutes and Ordinances (annually).

The University of Cambridge Guide to Courses (annually: online only from 2007-8).

The Cambridge Pocket Diary (annually).

Index

Inside back cover

Elizabethan Cambridge: George Braun's plan of Cambridge dating from 1575 (top), and John Hammond's drawing of 1592. Many of today's familiar landmarks are already in place, and the main street system is more or less the same. Note on the Hammond drawing the different layout of the courts at Trinity and St John's Colleges, and the Greyfriars' precinct of the Franciscans, where Sidney Sussex College now lies.

Images courtesy of Cambridge University Library